GREECE

GREECE

OTHON TSOUNAKOS

EKDOTIKE ATHENON S.A.

Publisher: Christiana G. Christopoulou
English translation: Richard Witt
Artistic supervision: Spyros Karachristos
Photo research: Georgia Moschovakou
Editor: Maria Koursi
Photographs: Studio Kontos, Antony Kalogirou, Vangelis Thelegos,
Elias Georgouleas, Ekdotike Athenon Archives
Cover photo: Spyros Tsavdaroglou
DTP: E. Varvakis Co.
Printed and bound by Metron S.A. - Ekdotike Hellados

ISBN: 978-960-213-437-5
Copyright © 2007 by Ekdotike Athenon S.A.
13, Ippokratous St., Athens 106 79
Printed and bound in Greece

AUTHOR'S FOREWORD

It is not the purpose of this book to add just one more to the already huge number of general tourist guides to Greece, whether in Greek, English, Russian or Japanese. It is doubtful, indeed, whether such an ambition could ever be achieved in a couple of hundred pages and half that number of illustrations.

What makes Greece, as it has always made her, such an inexhaustible treasury of memorable experience for the discerning traveller, is the depth of Greek history, combined with her unique display of classical monuments, her fascinating folklore, and her abundant natural beauty. A full picture of these is not to be had in a matter of days or even of weeks. It is no exaggeration to say that even the experts on Greece, people who have spent a lifetime getting to know and describe in detail the main 'sights' of the Greek landscape, whether they are historians or naturalists, often have the happy sensation of discovering the country for the first time and being just at the start of their research.

And so this volume aims simply to be an incentive – a strong one, we hope – to the inquisitive voyager to Greece. Its purpose is to give her or him, so far as is possible, and with the assistance of carefully selected photographs of the best quality, a basic outline of the directions which she or he should follow in roaming the land; or more simply still, what not to miss.

Of course these are the author's choices, and therefore not free from bias, however hard one tries. But his criteria are objective ones, and in any case, as the classical Greeks observed, what mortal is free from error? As we hope the reader will appreciate, blinkered devotion to the ruins of antiquity has been curbed, and the emphasis has been adjusted to include the presence of Byzantium in Greece, to say nothing of more recent history. In any case, the aim has been to give the reader certain fundamental pieces of information for direction finding, enabling her (or him) to have recourse to onsite confirmation or to the specialist literature.

Methodologically speaking, the text follows certain constant principles that relate to geography and to the time-honoured administrative structure of Modern Greece, bar the latest subdivisions. Ahaia and Ilia, for example, are 'restored' to the Peloponnese, though officially belong to 'Western Greece'. The dromedary of Aitoloakarnania goes to 'Mainland Greece', on the same reasoning, while Thrace is treated as a separate unity, and not as a component part of 'Thrace-and-Macedonia'. And so on.

May this book be read with pleasure; and may it fulfil its intended role of 'being useful'!

Othon Tsounakos

Athens, view of the Acropolis from Philopappus Hill. The splendid monument in the centre id the Parthenon, built by Ictinus and Callicrates in the 5th century B.C. In the foreground is the Odeum of Herodes Atticus, where concerts and other artistic events are still held, in the summer.

SOUTHERN MAINLAND GREECE

PREFECTURE OF ATTIKI

The Prefecture of Attikí comprises the following: SE part of southern mainland Greece, a small portion of the Argolid (in the region
of Troizinia), the isles of the Saronic Gulf (Salamína, Aigína, Ankístri,
Póros, and neighbouring small islands), the historic 'Argolic' islands
of Hydra and Spetses (and neighbouring small islands), and, south of
Lakonia, the islands of Kýthira and Antikýthira. The strictly mainland
part of Attiki is washed by the Gulf of the Halcyonides, the 'Kingfisher Islands' (the eastern end of the Gulf of Corinth) to the west
and the southern Gulf of Evoia to the E.

The prefecture is about 65% plains. Its most typical lowland
extensions are the Athens Basin (lying between mounts Ymittós.
Pentéli, Poikílo and Aigáleos), the Thriasian Plain (at the centre of
which is the town of Asprópirgos), the coastal basin of Megara, and
the eastern plain (lying between Rafína, Spáta, Koropí and Markó-

*Athens, view of the Odeum of
Herodes Atticus, lying beneath
the Acropolis. The refurbishing of
the seating in marble was completed after the Second World
War, enabling concerts to be put
on in this theatre.*

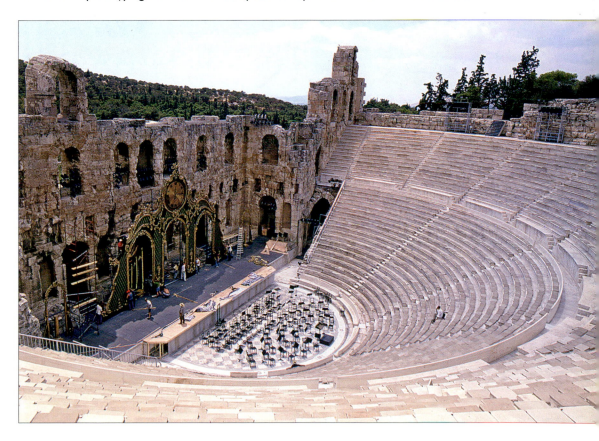

Athens, view of the Erechtheum, one of the temples on the Sacred Rock of the Acropolis.

Athens, view of the Ancient Agora (market place). This area was uncovered only at the start of the 20th century. In the background is the Stoa of Attalus, a postwar reconstruction by the American School of Archaeology and today the Agora's museum.

poulo and Porto Ráfti). Its highest mountain massifs are mounts Párnitha (1413 m.) and Pentéli (1109 m.) to the E and mount Kithairon (1409 m.) to the W on the borders with Voiotia, the Geránea range on the borders of the Attican portion of the prefecture of Korinthia, and mount Patéras (1131 m.).

The prefecture's river system is notably poor. The Kifisós is the one and only river, and there are no lakes to speak of apart from lake Marathónas, which provides the capital with water. The climate is healthy and temperate, despite the many unfortunate changes

which have resulted from unreflecting human exploitation – particularly in the Athens Basin and the coastal industrial zone in the W of the Prefecture.

Attiki (the classical Attica) is the hub of the country's land transport network. This applies both to road transport (with for example the Athens-Thessaloniki and Athens-Corinth motorways, and the peripheral Attikí Odós) and to rail transport (with for example lines from Athens to Patras and Kalamáta, and the Suburban Rail). It is also the home of the country's principal airport (El.Venizelos International, at Spata) and principal freight and passenger port (the Piraeus).

Whether speaking of geography, history, administrative, culture, or population, the prefecture of Attiki has markedly different characteristics from the rest of the country. It has, for example, a population of four million, the great majority of whom live in Greater Athens. We have therefore adopted a threefold division of the subject matter in the next few pages. First we shall deal with the urban plan of the Athens Basin, then with that of the rest of the mainland part of the prefecture, then with Attiki's islands.

Athens, the colonnaded Doric temple of Hephaestus. Popularly known as the Theseion, this temple stands in the grounds of the Ancient Agora and is one of the best preserved from classical antiquity.

Athens, the Monument of Philopappus, on the Hill of the Muses. It was erected at the start of the 2nd century A.D.

a. Athens and its urban plan

The centre of the history of the ancient Greek world is the history of Athens; and much the same is true of the modern Greek state. Though these lie outside the scope of the present book, it needs to be remarked that Athens came into existence as an urban centre in the second millennium B.C., to pass through the successive stages of being a kingdom, an aristocracy, a tyranny, and – at the end of the 6th century B.C. – a democracy. In the hundred years that followed, the city was foremost in repelling the threat from Persia and enjoyed an 'Age of Gold' – a period of extraordinary political and intellectual achievement, abruptly and decisively cut short by Sparta's defeat of Athens in the Peloponnesian War of 431-404. All attempts to restore the city to its former glories in the 4th century were a resounding failure, and Athens ultimately became a vassal of the Macedonians, to go into a rapid decline that continued, with rare exceptions, in the Roman period. By the start of the Christian (Early Byzantine) period and the reign of the emperor Justinian, the decline was complete. Thereafter, what had once been a mighty city was subjected to invasion from Western Europe and eventually from the Turks, to disappear, as it were, on the margins of history.

Athens, the site of the Pnyx, on Philopappus Hill. It was in this open space, above all, that the citizens of classical Athens democratically debated politics.

There was vandalism on a scale the city had never before seen, the prime example being the bombardment of the Parthenon by the Venetian general Morosini. Only with Greece's liberation from Turkish rule did Athens return to the forefront, when it was declared the capital of the fledging modern Greek state in 1834. From that moment on it never stopped growing. Building went on without rhyme or reason and the population swelled to gigantic proportions, particularly in the wake of the Second World War, creating many of the problems – such as atmospheric pollution and traffic congestion - that are still characteristic of the city today. Nevertheless, Athens remains a city with an unparallelled wealth of things to see, many places of beauty, and a personality all its own.

The principal group of monuments is the handful of wonderful buildings on the Acropolis, 'the Sacred Rock', as Athenians like to call it. It is here that you will find the greatest building of the ancient Greek world, the Parthenon. It was constructed in the 5th century B.C., by the architects Ictinus and Callicrates, the work being supervised by the artist Phidias. Other masterpieces of architecture on the Acropolis rock are the imposing entranceway of the Propylaea, the work of the architect Mnesicles; the Erechtheum, with its celebrated Caryatids; the little temple of Athena Nike ('Victory'); and the walls themselves. At the foot of the Acropolis, on the southern side, are the Odeum of Herodes Atticus, still in use for concerts, ballet and so on, and the Theatre of Dionysus, the place which saw

Athens, view of the Roman Forum. The Roman market place is on the outskirts of the Old Town, the historic quarter known as the Plaka. In the background (right) is the elegant 1st-century octagon of the Syrian astronomer Andronicus of Cyrrha. It is popularly known as the Tower of the Winds.

Athens, the Plaka. One of the numerous steep little streets of this picturesque historical nucleus of Athens, which runs round the foot of the Acropolis. Practically all the houses in the Plaka are excellent specimens of Neoclassical or vernacular architecture and are listed buildings, under the protection of the Hellenic Ministry of Culture.

the first performances of plays by the likes of Sophocles, Aeschylus, Euripides and Aristophanes. Near the Acropolis to the west are other important sites: the Ancient Agora, with its museum housed in the Stoa of Attalus, the impressive Doric temple of Hephaestus, erected in 449 B.C. and used by the ancient Athenians as a law court and administrative centre. Adjacent are 'Potters' Field' (the Kerameikos); Areopagus Hill, on which St Paul preached the teachings of Christ; the hill of the Pnyx, meeting-place of the classical Athenian People's Assembly; and Philopappus Hill and the Hill of the Nymphs, on which has stood since the 19th century the Athens Observatory.

To the N and E of the Acropolis rock is the picturesque old quarter of the Plaka, with its Neoclassical houses and narrow streets. On the fringes of the Pláka are a number of archaeological monuments including the Roman Forum. At the north end of the Plaka are the old Dimopratírio quarter, now always known as Monastiráki, and the Cathedral. At the east end is a broader site comprising the Arch of Hadrian (a Roman structure), and the ruins of the temple of Olympian Zeus.

If you then go back towards the centre of town, there are the open spaces of the Záppeion Hall, and the National Gardens, the main place where Athenians can stroll about. To the E of the Gardens, with its protecting hillock, is the Panathenian Stadium, venue of the first Olympic Games of modern times, in 1896 and in 1906. The National Gardens abuts on Sýntagma Square, the central point

Athens, Monastiraki Square. Set in the historic heart of Old Athens, Monastiraki brings together all the various historical and architectural elements that there have been in the city, over the ages: in classical, Roman, Byzantine, and Turkish times, and more recently.

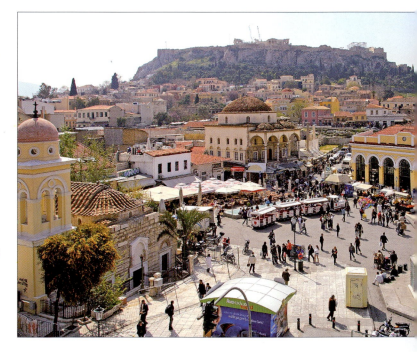

of the city, and is adorned by the large palace which now houses the Greek Parliament but was once the home of Greek royal families.

Leading away from Syntagma Square are the three great boulevards of central Athens: Stadíou, Panepistimíou, and Akadimías. On the first of these stands the Old Parliament House, and on the second the 'triptych' of the National Library, the University building, and the Academy building. Stadiou and Panepistimiou both go down to Omónia Square. The boulevard that intersects with them at right angles is Patissíon, on which are the imposing buildings of the National Polytechnic University and the National Archaeological Museum. Patission runs close to the extensive park known as Pedion Areos ('Champ de Mars'), Athens' second main 'green lung'. Some other large open areas in the city are Lykavitós Hill, with a picturesque little church of St George on its top, Stréfi Hill and Kolonós Hill, the Tourkovoúnia, the Botanical Gardens at Votanikós, and the University City site (Panepistimioúpolis). Athens has some forty museums, notably the Archaeological Museum, the Acropolis Museum, the Stoa of Attalus (with objects from the Ancient Agora), the comprehensive Benáki Museum on Vasilíssis Sofías Boulevard, the History Museum in the Old Parliament House on Stadiou, the Byzantine and Christian Museum, and the War Museum. The city's leading institutional bodies and organizations are the Academy of Athens, the National Art Gallery, the National Opera, the magnificent concert hall known as Mégaron Mousikís, the National Theatre,

Athens, view of the Kerameikos. This, the Potters' Field, gave its name to a whole historical district of Athens. It has one of the best-preserved graveyards in the classical Greek world, with tomb sculpture of rare artistic excellence and great historical interest.

Athens, Lykavitos Hill. This steep hill rising 217 metres above sea level is the highest point in Athens. On its summit is the picturesque church of St George. The hill also has an open-air theatre and 'soft tourism' installations. The summit can be reached on foot or by cable car.

Athens, the National Archaeological Museum. This is the country's main museum, with a wealth of important exhibits. Completed in 1889, it was extended in the period after the Second World War.

The National Capodistrian University, the principal higher education institution in Greece. The main building is now mainly for administration and ceremonies and conferences. The entrance (Propylaea) and the piazza in the foreground have recently been refurbished.

The Parliament building at Syntagma Square. What is today the Parliament Building was originally the palace of the first king of Greece, Otho, for whom Ludwig I of Bavaria had it built. It remained a royal residence until the mid-war years. After the Second World War it became the seat of the Greek parliament. The adjacent Tomb of the Unknown Soldier is also a creation of the mid-war years.

Athens, the Metropolitan Cathedral. This imposing edifice was built between the years 1839 and 1869, by a number of architects including Zezos and Saubert.

and the Municipal Cultural Centre. Of its very many churches, particularly impressive are the Kapnikaréa, Agiou Eleftheríou, and Agion Asomáton, to say nothing of the major Byzantine monasteries dotted around boundaries of the city with the rest of the prefecture (for example at Kaisarianí or Dafní).

The city of the Piraeus (population 176,000) is a modern creation. Its economic and social life centres on its great passenger and freight port, the largest in Greece. It has numerous monuments, enticing byways, and a considerable cultural life of its own. Of particular interest to the visitor are the picturesque little bays known as Mikrolímano (formerly Tourkolímano) and Pasalimáni (also known as Zia); hilltop Kastélla; the marine parade at Neo Fáliro, revamped for the Olympic Games, with the indoor sports and exhibition hall named (in the palmy days of Andreas Papandreou) the Stadium of Peace and Friendship. The other shorelines of the prefecture also have their attractiveness, particularly east of the Piraeus (Palaio Fáliro, Kalamáki / Alimos, Agios Kosmás with its extensive Olympic venues, Glyfáda, Voúla, and at the end of the line Vouliagmeni with its lake pool of the same name. Many of the citizens of Athens get their recreation in the greener northern suburbs, particularly in the district embracing Ekáli, Kifisiá, Pentéli and Melíssia, or on mount Ymittós, or at Haidári in the west, and indeed wherever there are parks, groves, and areas to stroll in or take an excursion to. A favourite jaunt is the area round the New Stadium (OAKA), at Kalogréza, venue for the 2004 Olympic Games, and the nearby grove at Nea Philadélphia.

Athens, the Old Parliament House. Dating from the 1870s, this palatial building now houses the National Historical Museum. The bronze equestrian statue in the foreground, cast by Sohos in 1904, is of the Revolutionary general Kolokotronis.

Athens, the katholikon (principal church) of the monastery of Kaisariani. This monastery played a not unimportant part in the life and culture of the Greeks from the last part of the Middle Ages into the Ottoman period.

Athens, the National Library. This splendid erection and the two adjacent buildings (the University, the Academy) form a sort of Neoclassical triptych in the very heart of Athens.

Athens, view of the Panathenian Stadium. This structure was rebuilt completely in marble, to replace an existing classical Stadium, for the requirements of the first modern Olympic Games (Athens 1896). It also served for the 'inter- calated Olympic Games' of 1906. Since then it has hosted many top-calibre international sports meetings.

Athens, the New Olympic Stadium (OAKA). Essentially complete by the start of the 1980s, it was enhanced, only just ahead of the 2004 Olympic Games, by the addition of a spectacular canopy by the Spanish architect Calatrava. It is the core athletics venue for the area.

b. The remainder of mainland Attiki

The favourite route for an excursion into mainland Attiki is along the south west or the east coast of the prefecture, and it is here that the most popular resorts are to be found. Beyond the city limits at Vouliagméni there are the now built-up seaside towns on the way to Cape Sunium: Várkiza, Agía Marína, Lagonísi, Saronída, Anávissos, and Palia Fókia. Sunium itself is the southernmost tip of the Attiki peninsula. Here can be seen the ruins of an imposing Doric temple of Poseidon dating from 450-440 B.C., and an adjacent shrine, also from the fifth century, of 'Athena of Sunium'.

If you continue N along the coast you get to Lávrion, with its two nearby classical 'industrial archaeology' sites – the silver mining area and, at Thorikós, the silver processing installations. Keeping close to the shore of the southern Gulf of Evoia, you then come to Daskalió, Porto Ráfti, and Vravróna (where you are strongly recommended to visit the atmospheric classical site at Kommeno Lithári and, a little way away, the excellent museum). After that you pass through Loútsa, the passenger port of Rafína, known for its fish, Máti, and Schiniás. You are now not very far from the village of Marathon, and very close to the mound commemorating the Athenians who fell at the battle of Marathon in 490 B.C. Next is the site of Rhamnoús, with a sixth-century B.C. temple of Nemesis. The final points north on this route along the Gulf of Evoia are Kálamos/Agioi Apóstoloi, from which the woodland classical sanatorium of Amphiáreio can be visited, and lastly Skála Oropoú and Halkoútsi.

If you strike inland, worth seeing are the 'Midlands' (Mesógia), with the Cave of Paianía; the lake of Marathon; the hump of mount Ymittós, with the monastery at Kaisarianí; mount Pentéli, with the monastery of the same name; and mount Párnitha, with its National Park and well-known Casino.

NW of Athens the area is less thoroughly geared to tourism, mainly because of the piling up of industry in the coastal zone, but there are nevertheless some sites of major interest to the visitor. These include the classical remains at Elefsína, with an onsite museum; the little town of Mégara, with its Fountain of Theagenes; and, on 'Kingfisher Bay' (Kólpos ton Alkyonídon), the seaside resorts of Alepohóri and Porto Germenoú. On the very borders of the prefecture there is much to be said for exploring the slopes of mount Kithairón and the pretty village of Vília.

Troizinia, the Peloponnesian district paradoxically annexed to Attiki, will be dealt with in the section on the prefecture of Argolida.

Piraeus. The small pretty harbour of Mikrolimano ('Littlehaven'), known in earlier times as Tourkolimano ('Turkshaven'), is one of the main focuses for the social life of the Piraeus.

The modern Piraeus, a city in its own right, was born at the same time as the fledgling modern Greek state, in the 1830s. Ere long it had become a thriving urban centre, thanks to its large freight and passenger port. This view is of part of the harbour, its main economic engine.

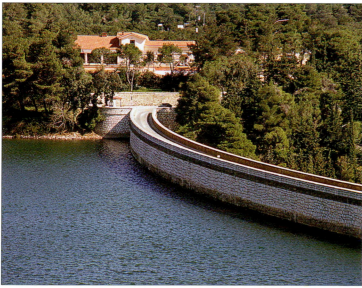

Sunium, view of the Temple of Poseidon, from the air. This colonnaded Doric temple, dating from the 5th century B.C., occupies a site of rare natural beauty, at the southernmost tip of Attiki.

View of the manmade Lake of Marathon. Constructed in 1925-1931, it was for several decades Athens' one and only supply of household water.

Aigina, the Temple of Aphaea.
Built soon after the Greek naval
victory at Salamis in 480 B.C.,
this temple replaced an earlier
one, and was dedicated to a
minor local deity. It is the island's
most important archaeological
site.

View of Paros. The island has
enjoyed a rapid increase
in tourism, largely because
it is close to the mainland
Peloponnese.

c. The islands of Attiki

The island closest to mainland Attiki is Salamína (the classical Salamis). It is just one mile from the Piraeus suburb of Pérama. Over the last few years the island has been rapidly upgraded. Its main towns are its harbour of Paloúkia, and Koúlouri. Excursions to the monastery of Faneroméni are extremely popular. There are nice resorts at Aiántio, Peristéra, Kakí Vígla, and Selínia.

   S of Salamina is the lovely island of Aígina. Its administrative seat and main port, also named Aígina, is a picturesque town that was the first capital of the new Greek state, in 1828-1829. Many of its historic buildings are still to be seen: for instance the Orphanage, built in 1828; the Eunardis building, dating from 1830, the very first higher education institute in modern Greece; the mansions of Kanaris and Trikoupis; the Government House which was the residence of John Capodistrias when he became the first governor of the fledgling Greek state on 26th January 1828; and the Colonna archaeological site, where the prehistoric settlement stood in the years 2500-1600 B.C. Aigina Town also has three museums: the Archaeology Museum, the Folk Museum and the Caprálos Museum. The main things to see on the island include the temple of Athena Aphaea near the seaside resort and harbour of Agia Marína, and the Colonna site. There are also many visitors to a monastery, six kilometres

The port town on the historic island of Hydra, showing its traditional buildings. Cars are banned on the island.

Spetses. This island at the mouth of the Gulf of Argos will for ever be linked with the history of modern Greece and the War of Independence. Here we see its little harbour.

distant from the main town, that was the home of a latter-day saint, Nektários. Two of Aígina's best-known resorts besides the town itself are Souvála and Agía Marína. Of interest, too, is the neighbouring little island of Ankístri.

Not far from the coasts of Troizínia is Póros, in mythology the island sacred to Poseidon, with numerous beautiful beaches. The most striking of its charms are its clock tower (1927) and a grove of lemon trees with wonderful views out to sea. There are an archaeological museum and a substantial municipal library.

To the south of the Argolid peninsula there is a group of islands comprising Hydra, Spétses and Dokós, all important in modern Greek history, and various smaller islets. The port town of Hydra is a most charming town, a conservation area. It harks back to the struggles of its seafaring inhabitants against the Turkish tyrant. The mementoes of those heroic days are the mansions of its sea captains, men such as Miaoúlis, Koundouriótis, Tombázis, Kriezís, and Tsamadós, and the harbour with its cannon and embrasures. Cars are banned on any part of Hydra. Similar interest attaches to Spetses, with in mid harbour its historic Dápia – the Old Cannonade, where the chieftains and captains mustered in 1821. The town also has its Neoclassical buildings, for instance Bouboulína's House and the Méxi Mansion, both of which are now museums.

Our journey to the islands of the Prefecture of Attiki ends with a voyage to Kýthira (to quote the title of a famous French Romantic poem). Kýthira belongs historically to the Ionian Isles, geographically to the Peloponnese (for it is S of Lakonia), and administratively, for reasons that are still obscure, to 'distant' Attiki. It is also Aphrodite's territory. This is one of the prettiest of all Greek islands, with rare natural beauty. It has picturesque seaside villages and hamlets. These include the main settlement (called Kýthira or alternatively Hora), a cluster of blinding white cottages with a medieval castle dating from 1503 on the hill above the village; Agia Pelagía with its gorge, Avlemónas with its Venetian castle in the harbour; Diakófti; Kapsáli; and Platiá Ammos ('Broadsands'). Further S still is the islet of Antikýthira, the classical Aegila. It was here that divers found two remarkable treasures: the lovely bronze statue, dating to about 340 B.C., known as the Young Man of Anticythera, and the celebrated Anticythera Mechanism, dating to about 80 B.C. The second of these is an elaborate and beautifully-made clock mechanism, about which various different theories have been put forward, both by scientists and by para-scientists. The statue and the clock are both now in the National Archaeological Museum.

Kythira. This island, 20 miles long by 12 miles wide, is an oddity in that it belongs administratively to Attica, geographically to the Peloponnese, historically to the Ionian Isles – and mythologically to Aphrodite! Its lush beauty makes it a paradise for outdoor pursuits. Here we see the main town (Hora) with its adjacent fortress.

PREFECTURE OF VOIOTIA

The Prefecture of Voiotía comprises the eastern mainland regions of southern mainland Greece lying between Attikí and Fthiotída, with the exception of part of the E coast (facing Halkída) which belongs to the pref. of Evoia. It is washed to the S by the Gulf of Corinth (Ormos Alkyonídon &c) and to the E, via small channels, by the N and S Gulf of Evoia.

The ground is approximately 60% plain, especially in the W. The highest mountain massifs are Parnassós, the highest peak of which (2457 m) is slightly into Fthiotída, and Elikónas (1748 m), the classical Helicon, in the SW. The southern coastal zone is in a strongly seismic area and exhibits a fair number of bays and inlets. The basis of the hydrographic system is the Boeotian Kifisós river, whose waters once used to supply lake Kopaída. Now that the latter lake has been completely drained, the waters of the Kifisós are mainly channelled into the Ylíki-Paralímni lake system, on the borders with the mainland section of the pref. of Evoia. It is this system that, together with lake Marathon, provides Athens with its water. In the

Livadeia.

S of the prefecture we find the river Asopós, which enters the pref. of Attikí, to discharge in the vicinity of Skála Oropoú.

Mount Parnassus, one of the most popular areas in Greece, especially for winter sports. This is a view of the Ski centre.

There is road and rail communication with the prefecture via the Athens-Thessaloniki motorway and the railway that follows the same course. The main interior through road passes through Thíva, Livadeiá, and Aráhova, connecting E and W southern mainland Greece.

The pref. capital is Livadeiá (pop. 22,000) in the NW, in the foothills of mt Elikónas, 130 km from Athens. The town was already well known in ancient times, because of the Oracle of Apollo Tryphonius, fragments of which are still extant, and because of the river Herkys with its springs of Memory and Oblivion. Over the centuries it was often the conqueror's prize. It was one of the key towns in the Greek War of Independence, being liberated in 1829. The principal site of interest is a 13th-14th century medieval castle on Prophítis Ilías hill.

Livadeiá is a good base from which to explore the N of the prefecture, where there are many beauties of nature and many sites of historical interest. Going from W to E, there are the mountain massif of Parnassós, with its National Park (which edges over into the neighbouring prefectures of Fthiotída and Fokída) and the picturesque hill town of Aráhova, associated with the revolutionary activity of Karaiskakis, a place well worth stopping to look at and with good tourist amenities. For those interested in the topography of monuments, a visit should be made to Dávlia, for the ruins of the classical city, a monastery of the Dormition, and other places of interest; to the archaeological site of the acropolis of Panopeus, where there are traces of very early Cyclopean fortifications; and of course Chaeronea, the site of the battle in which Philip II of Macedon defeated the alliance facing him, in 338 B.C., a turning point in history. The important things to see hereabouts are 'the Lion of Chaeronea', a huge memorial statue; a classical theatre hewn in the rock; and the Archaeological Museum.

E of Chaeronea is Boeotian Orkhomenós (pop. 11,000 approx.), one of the oldest towns in the Greek world, and the focal point of the Minyan civilization. It was sacked in 367 B.C. by the Thebans. Outsanding among the local monuments are the 'beehive' Treasure of the Minyans, an important tomb dating from the 13th century B.C. and the remains of a Mycenean palace, as well as the remains of a theatre and walls from a much later period, the 4th century B.C. In the same district is a historic Byzantine building, the 9th-century Skrípou monastery, with its ornate katholikon dedicated to the Dormition and to the Apostles Peter and Paul.

W of Livadeiá, close to the pref. of Fokída, is the tragic town of Dístomo, razed by the Nazi invader in 1944, as the War Memorial records. There is an archaeological museum, not far from which, about 10 km away, is another famous Byzantine monastery, Hosios Loukás. This is one of the major pilgrimage centres of the Orthodox world. The monastery was founded in the 10th century, by a hermit monk named Luke from Steira. Its impressive decoration includes a series of narrative mosaics of the highest artistic value.

In the NE of the prefecture, N of lake Ylíki, there are two major archaeological sites. One is the rocky eminence of Gla, which was once upon a time an island in the middle of lake Kopaída. This natural fortress was inhabited from at least the Neolithic period, and flourished in Mycenean and later times: it has Cyclopean walls and a complex of palace buildings. The other site is the classical city of Ptöon, in the vicinity of Akraífnio, inhabited from the 8th century B.C. to the Late Byzantine period: it has walls and an adjacent temple of Apollo Ptous.

Making your way cross-country to the south of Voiotia, the essential first stop is Thíva (pop. 22,000), built on the site of the classical Thebes, 45 km from Athens. According to legend Thebes was founded by Cadmus. It flourished in Mycenean times, and was to play a leading part in the great historical turmoil of the 5th and 4th centuries B.C., above all between the years 371 and 362, under its gifted leader Epaminóndas. In 335 it was razed to the ground by Alexander the Great; though rebuilt, it never regained the glory of its past. The town has much of interest, including a 14th or 13th century B.C. Mycenean palace, known as the Cadmeum; the temple of Apollo Ismenius; and the Cadmean Gates, dating from 315 B.C. Some 8 km W of the town is the celebrated Cabirium, functional

from the Archaic Age to the Proto-Byzantine period, with a large number of ruined buildings including a 4th-century B.C. temple of the Cabiri, a Hellenistic theatre, and a Stoa from the 1st century B.C. Not to be missed is Thebes' fine Archaeological Museum.

E of Thebes, towards the pref. of Attiki, is the township and archaeological site of Tanagra, with its tomb monuments and its typical terracotta figurines of young women in the height of fashion. Firther on are Schimatári (with an archaeological museum), Oinófita, and a number of smaller settlements.

All the S region of Voiotía W of Thíva is of great appeal not only to the archaeologist but to the visitor who is interested in nature or in sunny beaches. As you go from E to W your first stop will be at Platiés, the classical Plataea, on the lower slopes of mt Kithairón. This is a place whose history goes back a very long way. It was just outside Plataea that the Greeks faced and defeated the Persian army in 479 B.C., in a battle that was to be a turning-point in European history. The main items on the archaeological site are the remnants of the ancient walls; a temple of Hera (426-425 B.C.); the Visitors' Hostel ('Katagógeon'); an altar of Zeus the Liberator; and a mass grave ('Polyandrion') for all the Greeks who fell during the battle. There are also many Byzantine churches and chapels.

From Platiés you can go NW to Léfktra, another major battlefield, where a stone Trophy commemorates the decisive victory of Epaminóndas and his Thebans over the might of Sparta in 371 B.C.

The Byzantine monastery of Hoisos Loukas. This is one of the most important centres of pilgrimage in the Orthodox world. Founded by a hermit monk, Luke of Steira, in the 10th century, it has wonderful mosaics depicting scenes and figures from the Gospels with superb skill.

Arahova. This picturesque tourist trap is the main stopover on the cross-country route linking the east and west of southern mainland Greece.

Then on to historic Thespiés, in the vicinity of which was the Holy Wood of the Muses of Mount Helicon, with a theatre where, in classical times, the local people held the Mouseia, contests for musicians and poets. The tradition is continued in today's township of Thespiés, with its well-known folk festival: it also has a very respectable archaeological museum. The classical city's seaports were Creusis and Siphae; both these have an acropolis with the remains of ancient and later fortifications.

NW of Thespiés is Alíartos (pop. 6500 approx.), a town with a similarly rich historical past, being traditionally the place where the blind seer Tiresias and the general Lysander died. Today it is a hub of cotton production. SW of Thespiés is the pretty village of Dóbrena, and nearby the archaeological site of Thisbe, with fortifications and other remains of the classical city of the same name. Slightly to the W is the acropolis of classical Corsia, with walls and a temple of Hera. Further north are Agia Triáda and the nearby Cave of the Nymph Coronea, where interesting finds have been made.

Of the seaside resorts in the S of the prefecture, among the places we would suggest you visit are Kalamáki, Alyki, Paralía Saránti, Záltsa, Aspra Spítia, and Antíkyra.

PREFECTURE OF EVOIA

The Prefecture of Evoia belongs administratively to southern mainland Greece. It comprises the large island of Evoia (with its adjacent islets to the SW and SE, such as Stýra or Petalioí), a small portion of Voiotia on the mainland, and the island of Skýros (with its offshore islets).

Evoia is washed to the west by the N and S Gulf of Evoia, to the E and S by the waters of the Aegean, and to the N by the Oraía and Tríkeri channels that separate the Prefecture of Evoia from those of Fthiotida and Magnisía. The island is 75% mountain or upland. Sizeable areas of plain are those of Istiaía and Mantoúdi, in the north; Halkída with Psakhná, and Kými with Alivéri, both in central Evoia. The highest mountain massifs are Dírfys (1745 metres above sea level) in the central region; Okhi (1938 m.) to the S, and Kandili (1246 m.) to the N. Evoia's hydrographic system comprises little rivers and torrents (such as the Lilás, the Kiréfs, or the Niréfs), and in the central region lake Dýstos. The climate is generally mild and Mediterranean.

Evoia is linked with Athens by road, chiefly via the great suspen-

Halkida (Chalcis), the suspension bridge. This bridge, one of the major engineering works of the past few years, solved the thorny problem of adequate road access to the prefecture of Evoia. Prior to its construction, all traffic had to pass over the little double-action bridge across the Euripus.

sion bridge at Halkída. There are numerous ferry-boat services across both the northern and the southern Gulf of Evoia (for instance from Loutrá Aidipsoú to Arkítsa and from Stýra, Marmári and Kárystos to Rafína). There is a steamship service to Skýros from Kými, more frequent in the summer than in the winter months.

The Prefecture's capital and largest urban centre is Halkída (the classical Chalcis), a town of some 54,000 inhabitants 90 kilometres away from Athens. The main part of the town stands on the western coast of the ´Evripos strait, but part also lies on the Boiotian shore opposite. Halkida is a modern-looking town that retains many picturesque buildings from the past. Do not omit to go on to the bridge across the Evripos and watch the natural phenomenon of the eddying ebb and flow of its waters. Churches to visit are Agia Paraskeví (5th century) and St Demetrius and St Nicholas (both 19th century). Of the massive fortifications and other works from antiquity all that survives is a handful of traces, a fact that makes the Turkish fort called Karababá (actually in Venetian style, on the coast of Voiotia) of outstanding interest. The town has important museums of archaeology and folklore, and a substantial municipal library. It was the birthplace of artistic celebrities: Skalkóttas, Skaríbas, Orestis Makrís, Dimitris Mytarás.

A few kilometres north of Halkida is the site at Mánika, only partially excavated, where Bronze Age and later tombs and other monuments have been found. East of Thebes, at Kefalóvrysi on the far side of the village of Fýlla, a second settlement has been excavated, this time prehistoric, and again adding to our knowledge of the remote past. Close to Halkida, in the Voiotia sector of the prefecture, are numerous archaeological remains, notably the 5th-century B.C. shrine of Artemis of Aulis, witness to the vital historical importance of the whole of this region. To the south is Lefkandí, of great interest to students of Homer, where there is a long apsidal building (known as 'the Hero shrine') with grave monuments: it dates from the tenth century B.C.

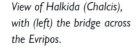

View of Halkida (Chalcis), with (left) the bridge across the Evripos.

Twenty-two kilometres south east of Halkida, on the coast of the Gulf of Evoia, is Eretria. The modern town is on the site of the classical city. This was one of the key places in the ancient Greek world: today it is a major summer resort. Noteworthy among the many things to see here are the ruins of temples of Laurelled Apollo (8th century B.C.) and Isis; a rotunda (5th century B.C.); a theatre of the same date; a wrestling-ground, a baths, and the House of the Mosaics (datable to 370 B.C.). From more recent times there is the house where Admiral Kanáris lived after the disaster at Psará. Many of the local finds are to be seen in the town's archaeological museum.

If you continue south east along the coast, you get to the pretty town of Amárynthos. In antiquity it was a cult centre of Artemis of Amarusia; there is a Macedonian-style tomb nearby. Today it is a summer resort with a long sandy beach. The next town is Alivéri, important because of its power station supplying the national grid. The district has natural beauty and there are various archaeological monuments, for example a Mycenean 'beehive tomb' at Katakaloú, excavated in 1907, and the Venetian fort at Dystos.

From Alivéri southwards, the coasts of Evoia are perfect for a summer holiday. The larger towns are Stýra, Marmári, and Kárystos. Karystos has ferry connections with Rafina and with the Cyclades; it is rapidly developing its tourism. On the sea front stands a striking Frankish castle, the thirteenth-century Boúrtzi; also of note are the town hall, the tree-lined squares, the warm shallow waters and sandy beaches.

There are again numerous summer resorts on the south east coast of Evoia. At the mid point is the small town of Kými, famous for its naval traditions. It makes a pretty picture with its broad central square, its stone houses, its flights of steps, and its pavestones. There is a fine Folk Museum.

The towns in northern Evoia – Nea Artáki, Psakhná, Politiká, Límni – are some of the prettiest on the island. By the sea is Roviés, and Aidipsós with its spa district of Loutrá attracts a great many visitors, having been famous from ancient times onwards for its curative waters. At Loutra there is also an archaeological display within the hydrotherapy complex. Further north is Oraioi and historic Istiaía, the economic hub of this northern part of the island. On the eats coast, facing out to open sea, are Elliniká, Vasiliká, Mantoúdi, Sarakíni, and a whole host of charming summer resorts. Inland, Prokópi and the adjacent monastery of St John the Russian are also very popular.

Skyros is the largest island in the Northern Sporades group: it is the only one that does not belong to the Prefecture of Magnisia.

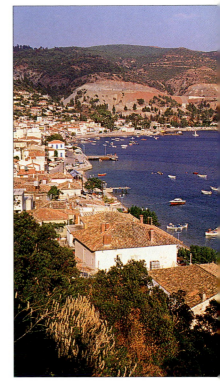

Limni, on Evoia. This is one of the most charming little townships along the coasts of north Evoia.

→

Eretria, the archaeological site. Eretria was one of the major city-states in Greek history in the pre-classical period. Among the now ruined structures on the site are two temples (of Laurelled Apollo, and of Isis), a rotunda, a theatre, a wrestling-ground, a baths, and the House of the Mosaics.

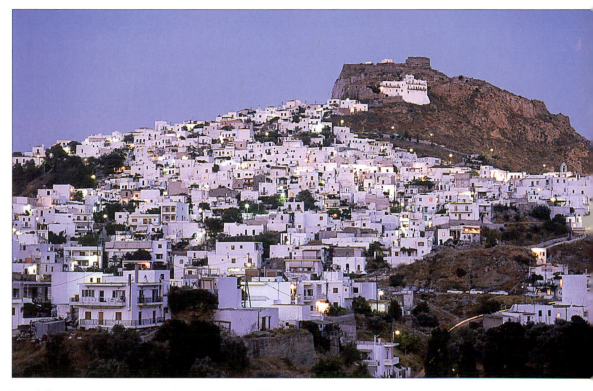

It is hilly to mountainous, with a summit at 972 metres above sea level. Its coasts are heavily indented, especially in the W, where there are a number of offshore islands (for example Skyropoúla, Válaxa, and Sarakíno). Its main town is Hora, on the NW coast, with a small airport close by. The island's characteristic houses, paved alleys, liveliness, and museums (archaeological, folklore) are a great attraction to visitors. Skyros (known in classical times as Pelasgia and Dolopia) has a very long history. Well worth seeing are the medieval fortifications of its main town, an extensive classical burial-ground at Magaziá a little way to the S, and a Byzantine monastery of St George, the island's patron saint. Many of its beaches are good for swimming (Atsítsa, Aheroúnes, Kalamítsa, Magaziá, Péfko) and the water is crystal-clear.

Skyros, view of the main town (Hora). The island belongs the Prefecture, not of Magnisia as might have been expected, but of Evoia. Among its attractions are the town walls, a classical graveyard at Magazia, and a Byzantine monastery (St George of Skyros).

PREFECTURE OF FTHIOTIDA

The Prefecture of Fthiótida comprises the NE section of southern central Greece. It is washed by the northern Gulf of Evoia and the Malian Gulf, to the E, and also by the Oraioí channel: these separate it from northern Evoia. The prefecture is about 80% mountain or upland, with the only substantial plain being the basin of the river Sperkheiós. The highest mountain massif is Parnassós, with the summit of Liákoura, 2457 metres above sea level, near the border with the Prefecture of Voiotia. Other major peaks to the S are Oíti and Vardoúsia, in the direction of the Prefecture of Fokida, and Timfrestós or Veloúkhi in the W, in the direction of the Prefecture of Evrytania. To the NE is mount Othrys, in the direction of the Prefecture of Magnisia; to the SE, are mounts Kallídromo and Khlomó. The main axial river is the Sperkheios, which runs through the prefecture from W to E, receiving the waters of numerous affluents, to discharge into the Malian Gulf in the vicinity of Thermopylae. The shores have many indentations, both large and small, especially to the SE, from Arkítsa onwards.

Communication with the prefecture is by road (via the Athens-Thessaloniki motorway) and rail. There is also a ferry to the coast

Lamia, Liberty Square. The town, now the capital of the Prefecture of Fthiotida, was once known as Zeytoun. Its present (classical) name derives either from Lamia queen of the Trachiniae, or from a figure of myth, a son of Heracles called Lamos. Its main attraction is its castle, where remains of the old fortifications can still be seen.

of Evoia. The interior road network is under continuous improvement, particularly in the mountains.

The Prefecture capital is Lamía (pop. 45,000), in the hinterland plain W of the Malian Gulf. It is 212 kilometres from Athens. Known in Ottoman times as Zeytoun, Lamía is named for Lamos, the son of Heracles by Omhale, or perhaps for Lamia, daughter of Poseidon and queen of the women of Trachis. In antiquity it was often at the centre of events, as for example during the Lamian War of 323-322 B.C. In Medieval and later times it was to become a Frankish and Ottoman conquest. It was liberated from Turkish rule in 1832. The town's archaeological museum is in the castle, parts dating to the fifth century B.C. There is an operational municipal library, with important early editions; also a folklore collection and an ethnographic collection. Seven kilometres away is the historic Gorgopótamos Bridge, scene of a famous exploit in 1942, during the Nazi occupation, by a combined force of Greek and British guerrillas.

Some eighteen kilometres SE of Lamía is Thermopylae. Today it is a flourishing spa town; in antiquity it was the site of the great battle in 480 B.C. between the Persians and 'Leonidas with his Three Hundred'. Close by, three kilometres away, is the Alamána Bridge, where, during the Greek War of Independence, Athanásios Diákos made his last stand.

From Thermopylae you have only two choices, to follow the coast south or to follow it north. If you do the first, you will come to the popular summer resorts of Kaména Voúrla, Agios Konstantínos, Arkítsa (where there is a ferry connection to Evoia), Livanáta (where there are the remains of classical Kynos, port for the city of Opous), and Skála Atalántis. A little further inland is Atalánti itself: it has an archaeological museum, a catacomb (named for St Athanasios), the church of Serafim the Holy, &c. If you do the second, you reach Theologos (the classical Alae, with important finds from the Archaic period), Malesína, and Lárimna (where there are the largest mines in Greece). According to tradition, this was where the Greek ships that sailed against Troy were built.

It is also possible to strike inland from the southern coasts of Fthotida and visit the many beauties of nature and historical sites at places such as the pretty town of Eláteia, with its classical acropolis and Mycenean burial-ground, Tithoréa, Amfíklia (the classical Dadi), Palaiohóri, Drymaía, and Madenítsa.

In the coastal region further to the north of Thermopylae there are many sites of interest. NW is the castle of Limogard (the classical Nathrakion) and close by the monastery of St Blaise (1746). Stylída on the coast is the port for Lamía: it stands on the site of

The monument celebrating the battle of Thermopylae in the Persian Wars. Here Leonidas, king of Sparta, together with his 'Three Hundred' warriors, met a hero's death.

classical Phalarae. Eventually you come to Akhinós, with a castle on the site of classical Echinus; the castle (Kastro) of Pelagia (classical Larisa Kremaste); and the seaside village of Glýfa, close to which are a 4th-century B.C. castle and an 18th-century chapel of Our Lady of Vavriní.

The northern and central hinterland of Fthiótida is also full of interest. Fifteen kilometres south of Lamia is historic Damásta, where there is a convent that played a famous part in the War of Independence. SW are Kostaléxi, the Oíti National Park, and Pávliani, a mountain tourist village 1030 metres above sea level. Eighteen kilometres W of Lamia is the well-known spa town of Ypáti, with its healing waters and its numerous medieval and other monuments, notably the fifteenth-century monastery of Agiou

View of the historic convent of Damasta. This women's monastery dedicated to the Virgin Mary is one of the major religious sites in southern mainland Greece.

Agáthona; then Makrakómi, where there are the ruins of classical Aeniadae, and Sperkheiáda, 240 metres above sea level and 35 kilometres from Lamia. In the far north of the Prefecture is the historic town of Domokós. It looks out over the Great Thessalian Plain; there are a medieval castle, standing on what was the classical acropolis, a cave (not yet fully explored) known as Koudounistó Pigádi ('the Bell Well'), and the remains of the 3rd-century B.C. walls.

Besides the above, all Fthiótida's mountain areas are highly suitable for outdoor pursuits and green tourism the whole year round.

Pavliani. This district in the mountainous hinterland of Fthiotida is steeped in history. It is an ideal destination for the nature-lover, in winter as in summer.

PREFECTURE OF FOKIDA

The Prefecture of Fokída comprises the S central regions of southern central Greece, north of the Gulf of Corinth. It is almost completely mountain or upland, with less than 3% being plains. The highest mountain peak in the Prefecture, and indeed in the whole of southern central Greece, is Gióna (2510 m.), in the central northern region. Other major peaks are Vardoúsia (240-6 m.) in the north west; Oíti (2152 m.) in the north, on the border with the Prefecture of Fthiótida; and the Lidoríki range (1911 m.) in the cen-

Delphi. 'The Navel of the Earth', as Delphi was called, was the most revered place in the classical Greek world. It was here that the federalist ideals of the Amphictyonic League were conceived, and that Apollo's Oracle performed its work. Here too were held the Pythian Games, one of the four chief sports meetings for all the Greeks. 'Essential viewing' comprises the colonnaded Temple of Apollo, the Treasury of the Athenians, the Altar of the People of Chios, the theatre, the stadium, the rotunda, the gymnasium, and the onsite Museum.

tral S region. The main axial river is the Mórnos, whose waters have been dammed to make lake Mórnos, a large manmade reservoir in the central southern part of the prefecture. The coasts are much indented; the deepest bay is at Itea, and has on its coasts the port town of Itea, in the nook of the bay, and Galaxídi, on the western shore. The climate is harsh in the mountainous interior, mild on the coast.

Communication with the prefecture is by road. However, the harbours of Itéa and Galaxídi are both accessible to vessels that are not too big. The road network in the interior is mostly in good condition.

Delphi, the Rotunda.
This architecturally innovative and very stylish Doric structure was built at the start of the 4th century B.C. Its purpose is still not very clear. As can be seen, it has been partially restored (in the year 1938).

The Prefecture's capital and largest town is Amfissa (pop. 7000). Formerly known as Sálona, this is in the central W region of the prefecture, at a distance of 200 kilometres from Athens. It is a town steeped in history, that has often been raided catastrophically, and that played a key part in the Greek War of Independence. The main things to see are the remains of the old walls (often destroyed and often rebuilt in the pre-Christian era); the mansions of two chieftains, Panourgiás and Dyovouniótis; numerous later mansions; and the nearby Byzantine church of Our Saviour (11th or 12th century). There is also an excellent Folk Museum.

SE of Amfissa, in a landscape of wonderful beauty, is Delphi, the 'Navel of the Earth'. This was the holiest place in the classical Greek world. It was where the federalist ideals of the Amphictyonic League came to birth, and where the venerable Oracle of Apollo continued for many centuries to provide counsel to all Greeks. Here, too, every four years, were held the Pythian Games, that great Panhellenic festival which included contests in music and riding.

Having suffered repeated invasion, catastrophe, and plunder, Delphi finally disappeared from sight, literally, in the reign of the emperor Theodosius, a zealous opponent of paganism, at the close of the fourth century A.D. Only in the late nineteenth century was it

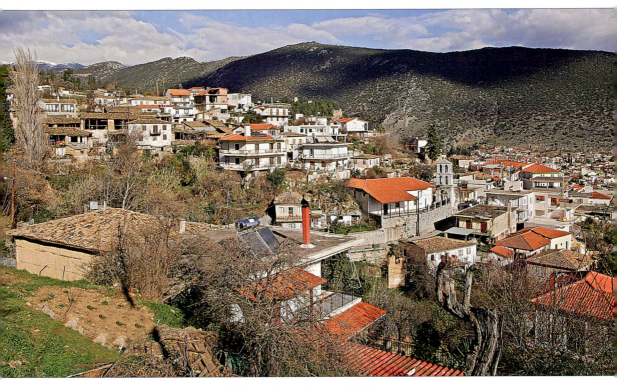

View of Amphissa. This town, once known as Salona, and now the capital of the Prefecture of Fokida, was to play a key part in modern Greek history. Among the things to see are the remains of its fortifications, the houses of two rebel chieftains (Panourgias and Dyovouniotis), traditional mansions, and the nearby Byzantine church of Our Saviour.

View of picturesque Galaxidi, on the Bay of Crisa. This historic township has a long tradition of seamanship, and was to contribute greatly to the success of the Greek War of Independence. Not far away is the 13th-century monastery of Our Saviour, where the Galaxidi Chronicle was discovered.

Itea. This substantial seaside town, the port for the Prefecture of Fokida, is a popular summer resort. It is also a good base from which to visit the rewarding nearby archaeological site at Cirrha.

brought back to the light of day by the (French) archaeologist's spade. Little by little what we can now see as the site of Delphi was excavated. Between the two Wars the theatre was the setting for the celebrated Delphic Festivals of the poet Sikelianós.

'Essential viewing' on the Delphi site are: the colonnaded Doric temple of Apollo (4th century B.C.); the little two-pillared Treasury of the Athenians (6th century B.C.); the Altar of the People of Chios (5th century B.C.); the Ionia Stoa of the People of Athens (5th century B.C.); the theatre (4th century B.C., but added to in Roman times); the stadium (5th century B.C.), where the Pythian Games were held; the Castalian Fount; the elegant Doric rotunda (4th century B.C.); and the complex of buildings round the Gymnasium, where lessons and sports coaching were given to the young. There is a fine onsite museum with finds of unique artistic interest: outstanding are the Charioteer, the Athlete, and the Sphinx of the People of Naxos.

Moving on SW from Delphi you descend to the pretty port of Itéa and from thence to Galaxídi, on the Gulf of Crisa. Galaxidi is another historic town, whose heyday was in the eighteenth and nineteenth centuries: it has a long and illustrious naval tradition and played a great part in the War of Independence. There are an archaeological and a naval museum, and an art gallery. Not far away is the 13th-century medieval monastery of Our Saviour, where the Galaxidi Chronicle was discovered.

Of the many other historic places in the prefecture, we would especially mention Lidoríki. This town 560 metres above sea level, former capital of the province of Dorída, paid heavily in blood for the gallant part it played in the War of Independence and in resistance to the Nazi invader (1941-1944). Graviá, in the NE of the prefecture, is another place worth visiting for its historical past: it was at the Inn of Graviá that, on 8th May 1821, the chieftain Androútsos and a mere handful of men kept at bay a whole Ottoman regiment under Omer Bryonis.

For nature-lovers there are the coast of Fokída in its entirety, the mountainsides of Gióna, Vardoúsia and Oíti, and the Parnassós National Park. The Park in fact spills over into the adjacent prefecture of Voiotía and Fthiótida, to which Parnassós properly belongs.

PREFECTURE OF AITOLOAKARNANIA

The Prefecture of Aitoloakarnanía is an artificial amalgam of two regions, Aitolía and Akarnanía. Not surprisingly, it is the largest prefecture in Greece. It comprises the western section of southern central Greece, though belonging administratively to West Greece, as do the Prefectures of Ahaia and Ilia.

It is washed by the closed Ambracian Gulf, to the north, by the Ionian Sea, to the W and by the Gulfs of Patras and Corinth, to the S. The Prefecture is about 80% mountain or upland: the only substantial area of plain is that lying to the SW and including the towns of Agrínio, Missolónghi, and Aitolikó and the outflow of the river Ahelöos. The highest mountain massif is Panaitolikó (1924 m.), in the direction of the Prefecture of Evrytania. Other major peaks are the Váltos and Makrynóros ranges to the N, in the direction of the Prefecture of Arta; the mountains of Nafpaktía and mount Arákynthos to the SE; and the Akarnaniká range to the W. The shoreline is often indented with inlets large and small, especially on the south west coasts where they have silted up, resulting in the Lagoon of Missolónghi, the 'enclosed sea' of Aitolikó, and a large number of islets.

The suspension bridge that links Rio and Antirrio, thus also linking the Peloponnese and southern mainland Greece. Opened to traffic on the very eve of the 2004 Olympic Games, it is one of the greatest technical triumphs in modern Greek history.

Missolonghi, the Marko Botsaris monument in the heroes' Park, represents the rebirth of Greece.

Missolonghi, a fish farm on the Lagoon. The area has the best known and most productive fisheries in the whole of mainland Greece.

The W coast has harbourages at Astakós, Mýtika, Pálairos and Agios Nikólaos, and the N coast (on the Ambracian Gulf) at Vónitsa, Loutráki, and Amfilokhía.

The hydrographic system is one of Greece's best. It includes the rivers Ahelöos and Mórnos, with their tributaries, the natural lakes Trikhonída (the biggest), Lysimakhía, Ozeros, Amvrakía, and Voulkariá, and the artificial lakes of Kastráki-Strátos, in the E central region, and Kremastón, in the NE, in the direction of the Prefecture of Evrytania.

The coasts of Aitoloakarnania have a mild climate, which changes to continental in the mountain regions of the hinterland, with heavy rainfall and snowfall.

Access from Athens by road is usually via the Athens-Patras motorway, crossing over the new suspension bridge at Rio-Antírrio. It is however possible to use the cross-country route through southern central Greece, via Livadeiá, Delphi, Náfpaktos, Missolónghi, and Agrínio. There is also a road link with Epirus, principally via the Áktio-Préveza undersea tunnel.

Missolonghi (pop. 17,000), though not the prefecture's largest town, is its capital. At a distance of 45 kilometres from Patras and 245 kilometres from Athens, the town stands on the Lagoon of

Missolonghi, on the south coast of the prefecture. It first became well known in 1571, thanks to the battle of Lepanto. Later, it was play a heroic part in the Greek War for Independence from the Turks, winning international recognition as a result of two events: the Great Sortie of its besieged, in 1826, and the death here of Lord Byron, in 1824. The town was rebuilt in 1829, and was given the accolade of the description 'Holy' in 1837. Chief among its monuments are the Hero Shrine (or Grave of the Heroes), erected in 1829, where there are the graves and busts of Greek and Philhellene warriors such as Botsaris and Byron; the Tomb of the Heroes; and the Gate of the Sortie, built in 1839. There are also the remains of the old fortifications; the Town Hall, in which are a picture gallery and a fascinating collection of memorabilia connected with the War of Independence; the family homes of the poet Palamás and the statesman Trikoúpis; and the Library. And of course there is the Lagoon and its many eyots, formed by silting and rich in fisheries: to the north it runs out in the Lagoon of the picturesque town of Aitolikó, built entirely on a small flat island.

East of Missolonghi can be seen the remains of a shrine of Artemis Laphria and Apollo Laphrius, an important Aitolian temple, the heyday of which was in the sixth century B.C.; and the Hero

Antirrio, the fortifications. This impressive sight is the first that greets the traveller leaving the Peloponnese for mainland Greece.

View of Nafpaktos, with its forti-fied harbour. Not only has the town its historical monuments; it is also a magnet to summer visi-tors and an excellent base from which to explore the beautiful countryside of Nafpaktos' moun-tainous hinterland.

Shrine of the Calydonian Lion, dating from 1000 B.C. There is also the Pantaxiótissa monastery, with its 10th-century Middle Byzantine katholikon (principal church) of the Dormition.

Next comes Antírrio, at one end of the mighty suspension bridge, very nearly three kilometres long, that links southern mainland Greece with the Peloponnese and parts the Gulf of Patras from the Gulf of Corinth. You then arrive at Náfpaktos (pop. 13,000). This town's history dates from the classical period. Its haughty castle stands on the site of the classical acropolis, while there were successive changes to the fortifications from antiquity to the Turkish period. Náfpaktos is ideal for a summer holiday, and also a good base from which to explore the mountainous hinterland of Nafpaktía, with its beautiful scenery and its many picturesque little villages steeped in history, no more than thirty to eighty kilometres from the town (places such as Plátanos, Upper and Lower Hóra, Tríkorfo, Ambelakiótissa, or Elatoú).

W of Nafpaktia there is the archaeological site of Thermon to be visited. This was an important place for the ancient Aitolians, in terms of religion and politics. On the site are the remains of prehistoric buildings; and of a classical temple of Apollo Thermius, a council chamber, a fountain. You next come to the lake system of Trikhonída and Lysimakhía, a particularly interesting wetland. N of it

is Agrínio (or Vrahóri, as it was known in the Turkish period), the largest town in the prefecture (pop. 52,000). It flourished in Turkish times, but paid heavily for its part in the War of Independence. Attractions include the Papastrátos Library and Park; the ruins of a 12th-century Byzantine castle; and the little wood named for St Christopher. The Archaeological Museum has exhibits ranging from prehistoric times to the Roman period. North west is Stratos, an archaeological site with a 4th-century B.C. temple of Zeus Stratius.

It is then possible to go onwards via the neighbouring lakes of 'Ozeros and Amvrakía, and the picturesque village of Katoúna, to the Ambracian Gulf. Your first stop will be at Amfilokhía (once known as Karvasarás), founded by Ali Pasha. This town (pop. 5000), no great distance from the site of Amphilochian Argos, lies 80 kilometres from Missolonghi. NW is another seaside town, Vónitsa (pop. 4000). Founded in the fourth century A.D., it was no stranger to history in the medieval and modern periods. Just ten kilometres beyond Vónitsa are lake Voulkariá, in which there is a submerged town, and the rewarding archaeological museum at Thýrreio.

The W part of Aitoloakarnanía has much to offer the visitor by way of natural beauty and historical interest, from the headland of

Amfilokhia. This popular summer resort lies on the Ambracian Gulf.

Aktio (off which took place the famous sea battle of Actium, Octavian versus Antony and Cleopatra) to the site of Oeniadae (in the SW of the prefecture, close to Missolonghi). In the course of this journey you will come to the charming seaside town of Astakós ('Lobster'), fifty km from Missolonghi and sixty from Agrínio. Nearby is the 'Cyclops' Cave' and seven kilometres away is the 15h-century monastery of Prophet Elijah, used by the Revolutionary general Karaiskákis as his headquarters.

Finally, you might like to explore the mountains in the N of the prefecture (the Váltos range and the Vale of Váltos, mount Makrynóros, &c), a memorable experience for all who love nature.

View of lake Trikhonida. Like southwest mainland Greece in general, the prefecture in which Trikhonida lies is well supplied with small lakes and with large rivers, for instance the Ahelöos, the Evenos, and lake Mornos.

PREFECTURE OF EVRYTANIA

Once upon a time the Prefecture of Evrytanía was simply a province of the Prefecture of Aitoloakarnanía. It comprises the NW regions of southern central Greece, and is the only prefecture of this Division that is landlocked.

It is entirely mountainous, a spur of the Píndos range. Its highest massifs are Timfrestós (2315 m.), also known as Veloúkhi, on the border with the Pref. of Fthiótida; and the mountain complex of the Eurytanian Ágrafa (2163 m.). The main axial river is the Ahelöos, which marks off Evrytania from Aitoloakarnania, forming the large manmade lake of Kremastón. The lake receives the waters of the rivers Agrafiótis, Mégdovas (also known as Tavropós), and Trikeriótis (a river formed by the confluence of two others, the Karpenisiótis and the Krikellopótamos). The climate is distinctly harsh, with very cold winters and fresh summers. This makes for a fine growth of thick forests, in which live many different bird and mammal species.

Communications and access to the Prefecture of Evrytanía are only by road, via the Athens - Thessaloniki motorway, turning

Karpenisi. This town, capital of the Prefecture of Evrytania, stands on the slopes of mount Timfrestos. It affords opportunities for a variety of rambles and scrambles in the hills around, with their rugged landscapes, extensive forests, and numerous historic villages.

Koryskhades. This village steeped in history will for ever be a name associated with the fortunes of modern Greece. It was here, in the village school, that the Political Council for National Liberation met during the dark years of Turkish rule.

The historic monastery of Our Lady of Brousos. This is a major pilgrim destination of the Orthodox world, with many thousands of visitors annually.

off on to the Lamía-Karpenísi local road at a point 295 kilometres from Athens and 385 kilometres from Thessaloniki.

The Prefecture of Evyrtanía is one of the most inviting tourist destinations in Greece. This is largely because of its great natural beauty. It has rugged mountain terrain, extensive forests, and delightful villages. The local people have all the traditional hospitality of their region. Thousands of visitors arrive, in the winter as in the summer months.

Evrytania's administrative seat and only sizeable town (pop. 7000) is Karpenísi (960 metres above sea level). It has played a major part at any time when the Greeks have been fighting for liberation. Standing on the slopes of mount Timfrestós, Karpenísi is an ideal base from which to explore the region. Your first steps may well be to the Ski Centre on Veloúkhi. Then there is Kefalóvryso, with its plane trees and purling waters, a wonderful place to unwind. To the S of Karpenísi there are many pretty villages steeped in history: Klafsio (where there is a 6th-century church dedicated to St Leonid, with a superb mosaic floor), Koryskhádes with its paved square and stone school building, Voútyro ('Butter'), the pair of Mikró Horió and Megálo Horió, and picturesque Kríkello.

The run via Domnítsa, Koumarísta, and Mesokómi takes you to

a magnificently wild landscape where the Pantavrékhei ('It Always Rains') Gorge is a most beautiful walk. After Megálo Horió you should visit the historic monastery of Our Lady of Prousós, which receives some ten thousand pilgrims every year. You can then follow the route via Fidákia, Agia Vlachérna, Vamvakiés and Ambélia. This will take you across the bridge over the river Trikeriótis, and through a little ravine and fine lush scenery with the sound of running water, before reaching the imposing manmade lake of Kremastón.

NW of Karpenísi is historic Víniani, with its iron bridge at Tavropós, the venue for extreme sports, and its stone bridge four kilometres to the east, a historical monument. Further north are a large number of other historic villages full of the promise of memorable rambles amid nature: for instance Valaóra, Monastiráki, Ágrafa, Metaxádes, Volári, and Granítsa.

A view of the great lake of Kremaston. This manmade lake is the result of damming at the border between the Prefectures of Evrytania and Aitoloakarnania. It marks the confluence of a system of four rivers: the Ahelöos, the Agrafiotis, the Megdovas, and the Trekeriotis.

PELOPONNESE

PREFECTURE OF KORINTHIA

The prefecture of Korinthía comprises the NE corner of the Peloponnese plus a small part of the Geraneia foreland, which lies on the far side of the Isthmus and belongs, geographically speaking, to Attica. The prefecture's shores are washed by the Gulf of Corinth, to the N, and the Saronic Gulf, to the E. These two gulfs are connected by the celebrated Corinth Canal. Cut in the years 1882-1893, the Canal is arguably the most important technical feat in modern Greek history.

Four fifths of the prefecture is mountain or upland, with the flat ground limited to the coastal plain. The principal mountain peaks lie in the W: Kyllíni (2376 m), also known as Zíria; and Helmós (2018 m where it lies within the prefecture). The latter is the mountain in which the Aroáneia range runs out, and it forms a single massif with Olígirtos (1935 m) and Saïtás (1814 m). These four mountain peaks frame the Feneós plateau, a broad and fertile plain. At its S end is the Stymphalian Lake (Límni Stymfalía).

At a lower elevation is the rump of east Korinthía. On its border with the pref. of Argolída, this runs out in a number of heights, notably the Megavoúni-Tríkorfo massif, cloven by the historically important Pass of Dervenáki. Also mountainous is the region on the far side of the Isthmus, frowned on by the majestic brow of the Geraneian heights. The shoreline of the Gulf of Corinth is mostly regular, whereas along the Saronic Gulf there are many little inlets. This is a coast with numerous beaches and much tourist development. The prefecture's system of rivers and lakes is far from rich, but does include a fair number of seasonal torrents. By and large the local climate is by and mild and Mediterranean, with the expected variations between the coastal plain and the hilly interior.

Communication with the prefecture by road is via the new motorway or by the Old National Road, both of which run from Athens to Patras, and via the Athens-Tripoli motorway. Communication by train is by the old Athens-Patras line or by the brand-new Spata-Athens-Corinth fast suburban rail link.

The prefectural capital is Corinth (pop. approx. 30,000). Set in the bend of the Gulf of Corinth at its south eastern corner, it is 84 km from Athens. It is a relatively new town, built in 1858 after a catastrophic *earthquake* destroyed the old town. It has a flourishing economy, and among its attractions should be noted the Folk Museum and the impressive cathedral church of *Paul the Apostle* (St

View of Ancient Corinth, from the top of the Acrocorinth.

View of modern Corinth. This is a relatively new town, founded in 1858, after a catastrophic earthquake had demolished the older town. Places to visit are the Folk Museum and the impressive cathedral church of St Paul (who preached in Corinth).

The Corinth Canal. Linking the Saronic Gulf with the Gulf of Corinth, it at the same time cuts the Peloponnese off, literally, from the remainder of mainland Greece. It was built in the years 1882-1893 and is an astonishing feat of civil engineering, perhaps the most remarkable in Greece.

Paul's). Of special interest are the ruins of the classical city at Ancient Corinth, 9 km south east of the modern town. Here are the remains of a *temple of Apollo* – one of the major edifices of classical Greece, dating from the third quarter of the 6th c. BC – and numerous other ruins of the classical and later periods. These include the *Pirenian Spring*, which was still in use at the end of the 19th century; half a dozen Roman temples; the *Basilica Iulia*, also Roman; and the remains of a 4th-c. *theatre*. Not far (3.5 km) from the ancient city is the Acrocorinth, the massive outcrop (575 m above sea level) upon which stands the Peloponnese's largest and oldest fortress, a constant strategic factor throughout ancient and modern Greek history.

Visitors generally come to the prefecture for one of two things, the seaside or the mountains. The coasts of Korinthía are well developed for the summer tourist. Loutráki is a very popular tourist centre with spa baths, not to mention the 6th-c. *temple of Hera* and the modern *casino*. Then there are Periyáli; *Léheo* (with its remains of a sixth-century Early Christian basilica church; Melíssi; *Kiáto*, with the nearby site of Sicyón, dating back to the 2nd millennium BC, *Xilókastro*, and Dervéni. Of recent years there has been an ever-increasing number of tourist enterprises along the Saronic coast, both on the Geráneia foreland (at Ágii Theódori and elsewhere) and in the properly Peloponnesian part of Korinthía, where popular places are the villages of Ísthmia; *Kehriés* (the seat of one of Europe's earliest Christian communities); *Loutrá Elénis* ('Helen of Troy's bathing place'); Katakáli; and the Sofikó locality (classical Solygia) with its seaside hamlet of Kórfo.

No less rewarding to the visitor is Korinthía's mountainous hinterland, with its superb topography of rolling hills and the many beauties of nature it contains. Particularly worthwhile is the route S from Dervéni up towards Evrostíni and then on to the Feneós district between the peaks of Helmós and Olígirtos. Here the visitor will discover picturesque villages steeped in history: Tríkala, Goúra, Kastaniá. The tourist infrastructure is discreet, and these are ideal spots in which to enjoy one's summer or winter vacation. Further to the W are the remarkable wetlands of the *Stymphalian Lake*, famous as the site of one of the *Twelve Labours of Hercules*; the pretty village of Kaliáni; Neméa with its vineyards (which are open to visitors) and archaeological site including the *temple of Nemean Zeus* (330 BC); *Hiliomodi*; and last but by no means least, the *Dervenáki Pass* where in 1822 the Greek chieftain *Kolokotrónis* inflicted a crushing defeat on the army of the Turkish general Drámali.

PREFECTURE OF ARGOLIDA

The prefecture of Argolída (the classical Argolid) comprises E districts of the Peloponnese: the major part of the Argolic peninsula (though not Troízen, which belongs administratively to Attica) plus part of the mountain hinterland lying between the prefs. of Korinthía and Arkadía. To the W, the prefecture is washed by the Saronic Gulf, and to the S by the Gulf of Argos. To seaward it embraces a group of three islands (Spétses, Dokós, and Ydra) which technically belong to Attica.

Argolída is four fifths (81%) mountains. Its highest massif is Olígyrtos, on the border with the pref. of Korinthía. Argolída's other major peaks in this region are Trahy Óros ('Hard Mountain'), in the direction of Korinthía, and the Lyrkeio-Artemísio complex, in the direction of Arkadía. The E of the pref. is dominated by the imposing mass of Aráhnaio Óros ('Spider Mountain'). The major flat lands are in two districts: at the crook of the Gulf of Argos to the N, where the towns of Náfplio and Argos itself are situated; and on the coastal plain in the SE, where the towns of Kranídi and Porto Héli are situated. The coastline is heavily indented, particularly to the SE. Though Argolída has a wealth of underground springs, the system of rivers

View of the Plain of Argos, from the citadel hill anciently known as the Larisa.

and lakes is impoverished, comprising only a handful of winter torrents. The climate has the usual variations between the coastal plain
and the mountainous interior, but can by and large be said to be
mild and Mediterranean.

Communication with the prefecture by road is principally via the
Corinth-Tripoli motorway: the tunnel piercing the heights of *Artemísio*
enables drivers to pass from Argolída into Arkadía. There is also a rail link,
the Peloponnesian line which goes by way of Argos after leaving Corinth.
Náfplio has its own bustling harbour, and there is also a sea link from
Argolída to the Piraeus, the coastal ships and hydrofoils that run by
way of Aígina, Méthana, Póros, Ydra, Ermióni, and Spétses to Leonídi.

The prefectural capital, which is also its second largest town (pop.
approx. 14,000), is Náfplio (also found as Nauplion), situated in the
crook of the Gulf of Argos, 148 km from Athens. This town, which has
been continuously inhabited ever since prehistoric times, was over
the centuries often under the sway of foreign invaders. The last to
occupy it were the Venetians, under whom the town flourished greatly, and the Ottoman Turks. Once Náfplio gained its freedom, it proved
a worthy capital for the fledgling Greek state: it was the venue for the
provisional governments of Count Capodístria (from 1828 to 1831)
and the Regency (from 1833 to 1834). Its streets will hold your interest continuously. There is the *Old Town*, a fascinating place to walk
through with its Venetian balconies, its Turkish fountains, and its elegant neo-classical houses. You can pause by the little chapel of *Ágios
Spyrídon* (1831), in the side street where Capodístria was murdered
on his way to church, or in Náfplio's own *Syntagma Square*, with its
atmosphere of an Italian piazza. You can walk along the charming sea
front known as the *Arvanitiá*. Or you can visit the town's citadel, the
Akronafplía (Acronauplia), with its fortifications dating from the 2nd
century BC, and go on up to the *Palamídi*, the Venetian fort, which is
still in excellent repair. The choice is between driving to the top, or
climbing eight hundred and fifty seven steps. You can also go across by
motor boat to the little island in the bay, known as the *Boúrtsi*, and
explore the tiny *Venetian fort* (1471), the town's mascot. Náfplio also
contains a number of first-rate museum collections: an *Archaeological
Museum*, a *Folk Museum*, a *Children's Museum*, a *Costume Museum*, a *War
Museum*, and even a *Museum of Komvolói* (in English, 'worry-beads').

In the NE of the prefecture is Árgos (pop. approx. 25,000), its
largest town. This is a very ancient foundation, celebrated in myth
and history. Its political and cultural heyday was the period from the
7th to the 6th century BC. You will discover numerous reminders
of its famous past. There is for example the hill on which its acropolis stands. This is still called by its age-old name 'the *Lárisa*' and is
topped by a 6th century BC fortress. There are an ancient *theatre*

*View of Mycenae from the air.
This legendary ancient city gave
its name to a whole way of life,
the 'Mycenean civilization'.*

*Mycenae, the 'Treasury of
Atreus'. This is the most impressive of all the so-called Mycenean 'beehive tombs'. It has
acquired the romantic nickname
of 'the Tomb of Agamemnon'.*

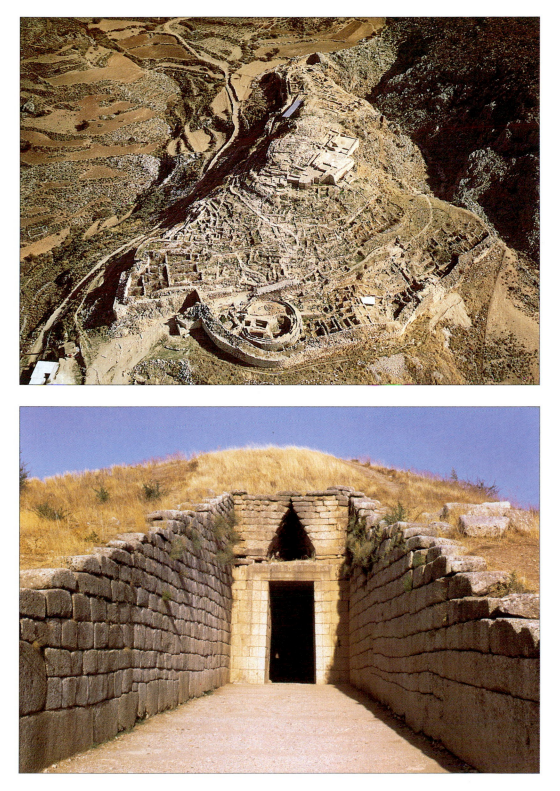

(4th or 3rd century BC), with an enormous auditorium hewn into the rocky hillside; and the remains of such major classical shrines as the *temple of Apollo 'Deiradiotes'* and the *temple of Athena 'Oxyderkes'* (Sharp-Eyes). Árgos also has an important *archaeological museum*.

Moving on N from Árgos you soon arrive at Mycenae (in modern Greek, 'Mykínes'), 24 km from Náfplio. The name 'Mycenean' is applied to what was one of the most noteworthy civilizations of the ancient world. Its peak was in the Late Bronze Age, from about 1350 BC to about 1200 BC. The archaeological site has such notable features as the 'cyclopean' (heavy masonry) *walls* of the acropolis, dating from the 14th or 13th century BC; the *Lion Gate*, a marvel of monumental sculpture, that was the original main entrance to the city; the *Palace*; and the 'beehive' (or '*tholós*') *royal tombs*, the most impressive of which is the *Treasury of Atreus* – 'the Tomb of Agamemnon', as it was known once upon a time – dating from about 1250 BC.

Between Árgos and Náfplio is Ancient Tiryns ('Tíryntha'). This major centre of Mycenean civilization was traditionally thought to have been built by the giants known as the Cyclopes. It has the remains of its Mycenean acropolis, including 'cyclopean' *walls* and what is a special feature of this site, a complex of *casemates* that served as passages in time of siege. SE of Tiryns is Ancient Lérna, one of the chief prehistoric

The Palamidi, at Nafplio. This excellently preserved Venetian fort is on the Palamidi Rock that stands guard over Nafplio. The climb is a stiff one, but rewarding.

sites in Greece. Lérna was the lair, so myth related, of the horrible *Hydra*, the serpent with nine heads that was eventually given its quietus by Hercules. Not far to the NW of Lérna is the *pyramid* at Ellinikó, the subject of much speculation of various sorts by archaeologists.

Pride of place among the classical remains of east Argolída must surely to go the *Theatre* at Epidaurus (in modern Greek, 'Επίδαυρος'). This is a triumph of acoustics. Built in the 4th and 3rd century BC, most probably by Polyclitus, it was extended in the 2nd century to include a smaller secondary theatre (*odeum*). In the 1950s, it underwent a complete overhaul. Today it plays a central role, every summer, in the *Epidaurus Festival*, when it is used for performances of

The Theatre of Epidaurus. This marvel of acoustics was built in the 4th and 3rd centuries B.C., with a concert room added next door in the 2nd century. It has been fully restored to accommodate performances of classical Greek drama during the Epidaurus Summer Festival.

Náfplio, the Bourtzi. Lying in the middle of the harbour, this little island can be visited by caique. On it is a little gem of a Venetian castle, which is now the city's emblem.

classical tragedy and comedy that thousands of spectators flock to from Greece and abroad. The archaeological site of Epidaurus contains many other reminders of antiquity. There are the *Asclepium*, the classical equivalent of a therapy centre; a *rotunda* (or *tholós*); the *sanctum* (where patients 'incubated' overnight); the 5th-century BC *stadium*; a *gymnasium*; a *concert-hall* (or *odeum*); a *temple of Artemis*; Greek and the Roman bath houses; and the *shrine of the Egyptians*, particularly dedicated to the healer god Asclepius.

Of the prefecture's many other areas of archaeological interest there is room to mention only *Asíne* (7 km from Náfplio); *Midéa*, with the remains of a Mycenean acropolis; *Kazárma* (14 km from Náfplio), with its acropolis and its Mycenean bridge; and Aliís (classical *Halieis*), a 4th century BC city with an acropolis, not very far from what is now one of Greece's most attractive tourist developments, *Porto Héli*. It is also worth crossing over to neighbouring Troizenía (administratively in Attica) and visiting the historic towns of Troízen, Méthana, and Galatás (opposite Póros).

The whole coastline of Argolída, it should be noted, continues to be a sought-after tourist destination in summer. Popular resorts include *Toló*, *Nea Kíos*, and *Ermióni*.

PREFECTURE OF AHAÏA

The prefecture of Ahaïa (Achaea) comprises the NW part of the Peloponnese: administratively it is classified as Western Greece. It is washed by the Gulfs of Patras and Corinth. Three quarters of the prefecture is mountain or upland. The principal mountain massifs are, to the E, Aroáneia, also known as Helmós, with the peak of Aetoráhi, 'Eagle's Back' (2341 m); to the S, mt Erymanthos (2224 m), also known as Olonós; and to the N, Panahaïkós (1926 m).

Areas of plain are confined to the NW part of the prefecture – the region of Patras and Káto Ahaïa and its hinterland – as a strip of land along the coast. There is a substantial system of rivers and lakes. To the N there are the seasonal torrents of Peíros, Gláfkos, Selinoúntas, and Vouraïkós. The first two of these empty into the Gulf of Patras, the last two into the Gulf of Corinth. To the south there are the r. Ládonas and the r. Erymanthos, both affluents of the Alfeiós. In the S part of the prefecture, near the township of Dáfni (also known as Strézova), there is a large man-made lake, the Ládonas Reservoir. The coastline is in general regular. The climate is variable, depending on the terrain: mild on the plains and harsh in the mountains.

View of Patras. The capital of Achaea has one of the best town plans in Greece. You should visit the classical Acropolis, the Roman Odeum (concert room), and the vast western European-style cathedral of St Andrew, patron saint of Scotland. Patras also annually plays host to Greece's principal carnival.

Kalavrita. On the right in the foreground is the War Memorial to those inhabitants executed by the Nazis on 13th September 1943.

The prefecture's capital, which is also the largest town in the Peloponnese, is the city of Patras, in Greek Pátra (pop. approx. 155,000), 220 km from Athens. Because it has a large harbour for freight as well as passenger traffic, Patras can properly be described as Greece' sea gateway to Italy and to the west of Europe. Looked at in another light, it is one of Greece's best laid out cities. It has straight streets that cross the lower part of town in a grid pattern; numerous squares; and a welcome breath of greenery.

Patras was originally named for Patreus, leader of those Achaeans from Sparta who settled here after being driven out of their homeland by the Dorian invader. Among the many things to see in the city are the 6th-century *medieval castle*, built on the ruins of the classical acropolis; a Roman *concert-hall* (*odeum*) of the 2nd century AD; the *cathedral church* of the city's patron saint, St Andrew (Ágios Andréas); the *Municipal Theatre* and *Public Library* (one of the biggest book collections in Greece); and the *Archaeological Museum*. Nor should it be forgotten that Patras is the seat of a *University* and also of colleges of advanced technology. It is also proud to hold what is the most popular of all the Greek carnivals: this takes place in February or March, and the centre of the festivities is the Plateía Ólgas.

If you follow the coast road out of Patras to the E, you will be able to visit the *Castle* at Rion, before going on to Aígio, with its celebrated church, the *Panaghía Tripití*, built on a rock. If you then go on to Diakoftó, you can get on the narrow-gauge mountain railway and enjoy the spectacular ride up to Kalávrita. This is an important name in Greek history, for it was here that the seven hundred local inhab-

Zarouchla. This delightful district in the hills of Achaea is well worth a visit for its incomparable natural beauty.

View of the historic Mega Spilio monastery. Dating to the 4th century A.D., this is one of the oldest monastic foundations in the Christian world.
In it is an icon of the Virgin Mary traditionally said to have been painted by St Luke the Gospel-writer.

itants made the final sacrifice, when they were executed by Nazi troops on December 13th 1943. At 4 km from Kalávrita is the historic monastery of the *Great Lávra*. Founded in the tenth century, by an ascetic monk from Athos called Athanásios, this monastery suffered repeatedly from acts of pillage and natural catastrophes. It is best known because it was here that Bishop Germanós, bishop of Old Patras (Palaión Patrón) made Greece's declaration of independence from the Ottoman Turks in 1821. A further 10 km north of Kalávrita there is another equally historic monastery, *Megaspílio* (the 'Great Cave'). This has the fourth-century icon of the Panagía Megaspiliótissa, traditionally said to have been painted by Luke, the author of St Luke's Gospel, and many other precious national and ecclesiastical treasures, including a large library.

Also worth seeing in this region are *Oriá*, with its Frankish castle, and the lake cave (Spílio ton Limnón) in the village of *Kastrí*. At *Vathialákka* there is the excellent Helmós Ski Centre.

PREFECTURE OF ILÍA

The prefecture of Ilía (the classical Élis) comprises a western area of the Peloponnese, and is washed by the Ionian Sea. A little over half of it (58%) is plains. The main mountain peaks are, to the NE, on the border with Aháïa, Erímanthos (2224 m), also known as Olonós; and to the S, Mínthi (1345 m). Its river system is extremely complex. In the N there are the Piniós, emptying S of Vartholomió; the Alfeiós, emptying into the Gulf of Kyparissía S of Pyrgos; the Néda, which forms the boundary between the prefs. of Ilía and Messinía; and, on the border with Arcadia, the Erímanthos, an affluent of the Alfeiós. Of its lakes the largest are the man-made reservoir on the r. Piniós, at the border with Aháïa, and lake Kaiáfa, north of Zaháro. The coasts of the prefecture are regular, and have no harbours. The climate is mild.

Ilía, one of the most rewarding parts of Greece for the traveller, offers a harmonious combination of historical interest with areas of natural beauty. The main attraction is, it need hardly be said, Ancient Olympia (in modern Greek, Arhaía Olymbía), the place where the

Ancient Olympia, with the Crypta and the Stadium. This site of the classical Olympic Games was specially brought back into use for the shot-putting event in the 2004 Olympics.

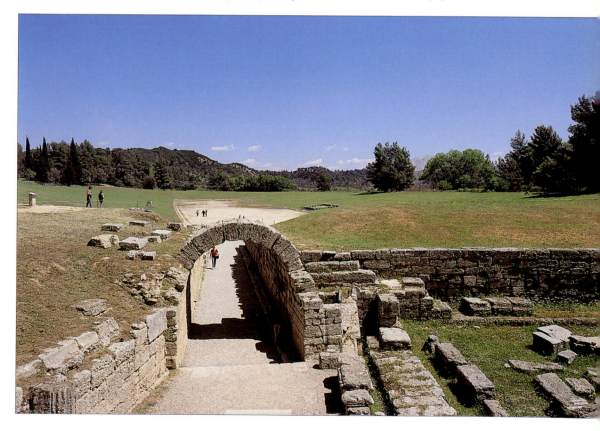

Ancient Olympia, the Philippeum, after its recent restoration. This building, dating of course from the 4th century B.C., was a tribute to Philip of Macedon, father of Alexander the Great.

Olympic Games was born. Olympia stands in a delectable landscape, the vale of the river Alfeiós. As you wander round the archaeological site, you can marvel at the *Stadium* and at what still remains of Olympia's other celebrated buildings – the *temple of Zeus*, the *temple of Hera*, the *shrine of Hippodamus*, the *council chamber*, the *shrine of Pelops the Founder*, the *Crypta*, the *Palaestra* (wrestling ground), and so on. Among the masterpieces of sculpture to be found in the on-site *Archaeological Museum* are the *Hermes of Praxiteles* and the *Nike (Victory) of Panionios*. And there is now a new *Museum of the Olympic Games*, in which you can see finds and memorabilia connected with the Olympics.

If you go W from Ancient Olympia, you will arrive at Pírgos (pop. approx. 24,000), 310 km from Athens. This is the prefectural seat of government. Pírgos is a relatively recent town. It contains a number of notable pieces of architecture: the *Public Market* and the *Municipal Theatre*, both by *Ernst Ziller*, and the attractive *Municipal Library*.

In the vicinity of Pírgos are some rewarding places to visit, including the nearby archaeological site at *Epitáli* (7 km); the pretty seaside resort of *Katákolo* (13 km); *Pontikócastro* ('Mousecastle'), a fort dating back to Frankish times; and, further inland to the E, the remains of ancient *Oléni*.

The prefecture's next largest urban centre is Amaliáda (pop. approx. 20,000). This town, of considerable charm, lies 19 km W of

Pírgos. It is an important agricultural centre. It has such notable Christian buildings as the *church of St Athanasius* and the two historic monasteries of *Our Lady of Francaville* and *Agíou Nikoláou*. Not far from Amaliáda are *Gastoúni*, with its twelfth-century church of the *Dormition*, and Andravida, which was once upon a time the seat of government for the Despotate of Achaea, and hence has the Frankish church, now in ruins, of *St Sophia*.

Northern Ilía has much else for the traveller to see. At 43 km is the district surrounding the port of *Kyllíni*, named Glarentza (Clarence) by the Franks. Here there are *spa baths*; a 12th-century monastery (*Our Lady of Vlachérna*); and the de Villehardouins' fortress of *Chlemoútsi* (Clairmont). Here too are *Vartholomió; Lehená*,

Bassae, the Temple of Apollo Epicureus. The architect of this elaborate, well-preserved structure was Ictinus, the architect of the Parthenon.

View of Lake Kaiafa.
This lagoon is in the south-west
Peloponnese, by the Ionian Sea.
It has internationally famous
spa baths.

birthplace of the novelist Karkavítsas; historic *Manoláda*; the lake behind the Piniós irrigation dam; *Ancient Élis*, historically important because it undertook the management of the original Olympic Games; and the village of *Lámbeia* (also known as *Dívri*), a rugged spot in which to enjoy the perfect summer or winter holiday.

A particularly attractive part of the prefecture to visit is the S area that was once part of Messinía. This contains a number of popular resorts. There is for instance the seaside village of *Zaháro*, on the edge of *lake Kaiáfa*, with its picturesque lake isle of *Ághia Ekateríni* and the spa of *Loutrá Kaiáfa*. Then there is the historic town of Andrítsaina, beautifully situated, one of the focal points of the War of Independence (1821-1829), and a hive of intellectual activity. At 13 km from Andrítsaina are the remains of the 5th-century classical city of *Alipheíra*. At 15 km is the *temple of Apollo 'Epicureus'* (410 BC) at classical *Bassae*. This magnificent building, still intact, was the work of *Ictinus*, architect of the Parthenon. There is hardly a day when there are not crowds of Greeks and foreign tourists flocking to see it.

PREFECTURE OF MESSINÍA

The prefecture of Messinía (classical Messenia) comprises the SW tip of the Peloponnese, and therefore of the whole of Greece. To the W it is washed by the Ionian Sea, and to the S by the wide Gulf of Messene. Approximately two thirds of the prefecture is plain or upland. This is mainly the case with the interior. Messinía is sheltered to the E by the Taÿgetos range, with the peak of Prophítis Ilías (2407 m) at the border with Lakonía; to the N by the mountains of Arkadía (notably Lykeo and Tetrázio); and again to the E, on the left leg of the peninsula, by such lower spurs as mt Lykódimou and mt Ithómi). The prefecture's coastline is mainly regular: its indentations are mainly in the W, in the small closed bay of Pylos. Messenía offers splendid beaches, ideal for tourism, mainly in summer. Its system of rivers and lakes is mostly impoverished. The principal waterway is the r. Pámisos, which empties into the Gulf of Messene. The prefecture's climate is mild and Mediterranean, with the temperatures never very extreme.

Communication with the prefecture is normally by road. The main access is via the central artery, the motorway from Athens to Trípoli, the highway from Trípoli to Megalópoli, then down to Kalamáta. The drive from Athens takes about three hours. There is at present a diesel train service between Athens and Kalamáta. The

Kalamata. Lying in the nook of the Gulf of Messenia, this culturally and economically thriving town has a large freight and passenger port.

View of Ancient Messene.
The classical site of Messene is
a good long way from modern
Messini; it lies on the slopes of
mount Ithomi. Ancient Messene
enjoyed a long period of prosperity, from the 4th century B.C. to
the 4th century A.D.

A section of the sea walls at
Koroni (Coron), on the east
coast of Messene. They are
basically Venetian.

The historic city of Methoni
(Modon), on the west coast of
the Gulf of Messenia. Its has a
fine medieval castle, one of the
best preserved in southern
Europe.

prefecture also has a civilian airport, midway between Kalamáta and
Messíni, and a sea link from Crete to Kalamáta.

A good place from which to start exploring Messenía is its capital, Kalamáta (pop. approx. 45,000). The town lies in the crook of
the Gulf of Messene, 238 km from Athens. It has a flourishing economic and cultural life, and a long past too, for it was already inhab-
itated in prehistoric times. There is much of interest to see, particularly in its two museums, the *Benaki Archaeological Museum* and the
Museum of History and Folklore. Among other places which you might
visit are the medieval *Castle* (where there are cultural events
throughout the summer, including an *International Festival of Dance*,
which is held in the open-air amphitheatre); the little chapel of the
Holy Apostles (now restored) in the commercial quarter of the town,
reputedly the place where the Greek War of Independence began
in 1821; the *Public Library*; the *Art Gallery*; and the *Old Town*, at the foot
of the Castle.

A large number of attractive tourist routes start from Kalamáta.
One of the most popular runs W into the *Messenian Máni*. It gives
fine views both of the coast, including seaside villages such as Vérga,
Kytriés, and *Kardamyli*, and of the impressive mountainous interior,
as seen in the landscapes of Taÿgetos.

A second route runs W via Messíni and Velíka to the west leg of
the peninsula and the district of Pylía. Along the east coast of this

Voidokilia Bay, view of the shoreline. This district is held to be one of the most beautiful in the Peloponnese.

leg are two popular summer resorts, Petalídi (26 km) and Ághios Andréas (38 km), and the historic town of Koróni (52 km), the medieval Coron, with its striking Venetian *Castle*. Of the same historical importance as Koróni, and in a comparable position on the W coast, is Methóni (the medieval Modon), again with an impressive *Castle*, one of the best preserved in the whole of southern Europe.

Further N, along the same coastline, is the Bay of Pylos – *Navarino Bay* – with the long island of Sfaktíria closing it off. Here it was, in 1827, that Greek independence was finally won, with the great *naval battle* of Navarino. Pylos itself, 50 km from Kalamáta, is a delightful little town with something of the atmosphere of a Greek island. Among the things to see there are the *Old Castle* (Palaiókastro); 'Nestor's Cave'; the Venetian *fort* of Niókastro and the particularly beautiful *Voidokiliá* neighbourhood; and *Maniáki*, where Papaphlessas and his brave men sacrificed their lives. If you continue N in this direction, you will come to three substantial towns: *Gargaliáni, Filiatrá,* and *Kyparissiá* (68 km, 83 km, and 68 km respectively from Kalamáta).

A third excursion takes you from Kalamáta to the modern town of *Messíni* and from thence N into the interior of the prefecture, where there are many notable archaeological sites to be seen. The most notable of all is arguably Ancient Messene, a city state which had its heyday from the fourth century BC to the fourth century AD. It lies at the foot of mt *Ithómi*, not very far from the village of Mavromáti and some 20 km from the modern town of Messíni. Also worth visiting are the many small townships in the hinterland, and the numerous tourist centres, of which *Androússa*, Valyra, Éva, *Meligalás*, Diavolítsi, Kopanáki, *Petalídi*, Artemisía and Finikoúndas are just a sample.

All in all, the prefecture of Messinía is a particularly inviting place in which to spend a relaxed summer holiday. Considerable efforts are being made to still further improve its hotels and related infrastructure, particularly in the areas along the coast.

PREFECTURE OF LAKONÍA

The prefecture of Lakonía (or Laconia) comprises the SE part of the Peloponnese. Two thirds of its area is mountain or upland. Its main mountain massifs are two: the great range of the *Taÿgetos* in the W, on the border with Messinía, with a peak at Prophítis Ilías (2407 m); and the *Párnonas* range in the E, on the border with Arkadía, with a peak at Megáli Toúrla (1935 m). Between them lies the broad flat valley of the Evrótas, the prefecture's only river of any real length, which empties into the Gulf of Lakonía. This gulf, a very large one, forms the coastline of Lakonía, and is bounded by *Cape Taínaro* and *Cape Maléas*. Its main feature is the great number of smaller bays that it is broken up into, and the same is true of the W coast of the prefecture, looking on to the Myrtoan Sea. The climate varies considerably, depending on the terrain, but broadly speaking is mild and excellent for the health.

Communication with the prefecture is by road. The main access is via a central artery, the motorway from Athens to Tripoli plus the Tripoli-Sparta highway. The drive from Athens takes about three hours. There is a secondary artery from Sparta down to Kalamata.

A good place to begin one's tour of the area is Sparta. This pleasant town (pop. approx. 15,000) lies in the Vale of Evrótas, 253 km from Athens. Refounded from scratch in 1834, it is a fresh, well laid out settlement. The past glories of classical Sparta can be appre-

Sparta, the Square. This little town with a great history is the capital of the prefecture of Lakonia. Laid out on a modern town plan in the 1830s, it is only three or four miles from Byzantine Mystras.

ciated by a visit to the town's Archaeological Museum, which is decently well organized and has a wealth of exhibits. You should on no account miss a visit to the ruins of the medieval city of Mystrás – "a Byzantine Pompeii", as it has been called – 6 km to the W. Founded by Franks in the mid-13th century, it was not long before Mystrás became part of the Byzantine empire. It held out against the Ottoman invader and was one of the last Byzantine possessions to capitulate, in 1460. A 'dead city' it may be, but as you walk its steep streets, admiring its superb secular and ecclesiastical buildings, you will be transported back into the past. Small wonder that every day literally hundreds of visitors arrive at its gates. Also worth making is the detour to the archaeological site of ancient Amyclae, 5 km SE of Sparta, which was reputedly the focal point, in remotest antiquity, for the civilization of the Achaeans, and after that for the Dorians.

At 43 km S of Sparta you reach Gythio, on the coast. This is a very pretty town with a long past, for it was already inhabited in prehistoric times. Today it is a bustling summer seaside resort. Gythio is a good base from which to explore the coast and find your own hideaway on some beautiful shore of the Gulf of Lakonía. There is the choice of family accommodation in one of the traditional stone tower houses or on one of the many camping grounds. Or you can cut through the middle leg of the peninsula, going SE, to arrive at Areópoli

View of the seaside village of Monemvasia and the peninsular Mount of the same name.

Gythion. This charming fishing port on the west side of the Gulf of Lakonia has its own jewel of an islet, Cranaë.

Vathia, in the Mani. Lakonia's tower houses of stone – fortified dwellings from olden times – are something of a trademark. They are seen at their best in the traditional settlement of Vathia.

Mystras, panoramic view of the medieval city and citadel. The nucleus was built in the 13th century. Mystras, the 'Byzantine Pompeii', was one of the last places to hold out against the Ottoman Turks, into whose hands it did not fall until 1460. It is a treasure trove of churches and secular architecture.

(72 km from Sparta), at the head of the *Máni*; the village of *Ítylos* (10 km further on); and the *Spília Diroú*, the 'Diros Caves', the world-famous underground system that was discovered only in 1958, by the Petrochílou's, when it proved to have been inhabited ever since the Stone Age.

The E leg of the peninsula also has much to offer. Its most popular site is Monemvasiá on the coast (95 km from Sparta), "the Gibraltar of Greece". This is a quaint medieval town built on a rocky offshore promontory – the islet known as *Laloúdi* – and looking out over the Myrtoan Sea. Like Mystrás, Monemvasiá consists of a *Low Town* and a *High Town*. The High Town is no longer inhabited; it contains a church (*Agía Sophía*) and ruined buildings of the Byzantine and post-Byzantine periods. The Low Town, with its perimeter wall, contains other notable churches – the *Panagía Myrtidiótissa* (1700), *St Nicholas'* (1703), the *Panagía Chrysafítissa* (17th century), *St Anne's* (18th century), and the church of *Christ Dragged to the Cross*. There is too a 16th century *mosque*, which now houses an archaeological collection. It was in Monemvasiá that the 20th-century Greek poet *Rítsos* made his home.

Further S still, right at the tip of Lakonía, opposite the town of Neápoli, is a small island called *Elafonísi* ('Deer Island') which has two superb beaches – Símou and Tis Panagías.

These popular destinations apart, you might consider exploring some of the less well advertised areas of this prefecture, inland as well as on the coast. You will be surprised how beautiful Lakonía can be, for instance on Taÿgetos or on Párnonas. Here and there is an archaeological site that few people know about. And there are the small townships which have played their part in history: *Skála*, *Molái*, *Krokaiés*, *Karyés*, and *Váthia* in the Máni, to name but a few.

Mystras, the Pantanassa church. This is an outstanding example of Byzantine church building.

PREFECTURE OF ARKADÍA

The prefecture of Arkadía (classical Arcadia) comprises the C and SE districts of the Peloponnese, and has no outlet to the sea. To the E, it is washed by the Gulf of Argos and the Aegean Sea. It is nearly all (91%) mountain or upland. Its most prominent relief feature is its central plateau, the *Plain of Tripoli* (700 m, on average, above sea level). The mountain massifs framing this plain are Maínalo (1980 m); a complex of mountains (Olígyrtos, Trahy Óros, Lyrkeio, Artemísio Kteniás) to the E, towards the prefs. of Korinthía and Argolída; and the N extensions of the Taÿgetos and Párnonas ranges.

To the E of this plateau is the Megalópoli basin, where there are coal mines. To the west this plain runs out in mts Lykeio and Tetrázio, and in Messinía. Other geographical units in this pref. are the mountain regions of Gortynía, W of Maínalo, and the SE district of Kynouría. The prefecture's hydrography includes a fair number of rivers; for example the Alfeiós, the Loúsios, the Ládonas, and the Erymanthos, plus the man-made Ládon Reservoir on the border with Ahaïa.

Astros of Kynouria. Its fine beach attracts many visitors in summer. Astros was to leave its mark on the history of modern Greece: an early Revolutionary Constitution bears the town's name.

Communication with the prefecture is by road (via the fast new Athens-Tripoli motorway or the old Athens-Tripoli National Road) and by rail (via the Athens-Kalamata line). The prefecture's main sea portal is Leonídio, where hydrofoils on the Argosaronic lines put in.

The capital of Arkadía is Tripoli (pop. approx. 25,000), 165 km

from Athens. This town was to see some of the greatest moments in the early history of modern Greece. Its capture by Greek revolutionaries from the Ottoman Turks, in September 1821, foreshadowed the eventual success of the Greek War of Independence.

Arkadía is a prefecture of great natural beauty as well as historical interest, and its tourist development has been accelerating to a significant degree over the past twenty or thirty years. On the road route from Athens, once you have passed through the tunnel and toll point at Nestáni, you are not far from the archaeological site of ancient *Mantinea* (12 km from Tripoli), where the city's Hellenistic theatre (4th century), council house, and temple of Artemis have been uncovered by the excavator's spade. Further N on the same road are the historic township of *Levídi* and the archaeological site of *Orchomenós-in-Arcadia*. If you are thinking of taking a winter break, you will enjoy wandering on Maínalo and its mountainsides, while the magical landscape of Gortynía, with its thick forests and its picturesque stone villages, is an ideal area to explore. One village that most people have heard of is Vytína, with its wonderfully healthy climate, its beautiful natural environment, and its excellent tourist facilities. The same can be said of the historic town of Dimitsána. Here you can see the childhood homes of Grigórios V, the martyr patriarch, and of Germanós Palaión Patrón, the bishop who was also a freedom fighter. Dimitsána also has a *Folk Museum* and a substantial *Public Library*. Also interesting are the old *Powder Mills*. At *Stemnítsa*, there is a notable tradition

Tripoli, the church of St Basil in the main square.

Dimitsana. Among numerous things to see in this historic town, capital of the district of Gortynia, are the family homes of two celebrated bishops (Gregory V, Germanos of Old Patras), the Folk Museum, the splendid Library, and the powder mills.

View of the Prodromos Monastery, an important pilgrimage centre in Gortynia, in the Arcadian highlands.

of gold- and silversmithing. Langádia is a town of masterbuilders. Karítaina has its celebrated castle. Then there are the many picturesque villages round about, each with its niche in history: Valtesiníko, Lykoúresi, Sévrou, Zátouna, Vlahoráfti, and the list goes on.

Other places worth visiting in the area are *Loutrá Iraías*, for its spa baths; the two historic monasteries of *Emialá* (1608) and *Philosóphou* (10th c.), each set in superb landscape; the archaeological sites at *Kamenítsa* and *Palaiókastro*; and, because it has developed into a major wetland area, the Ládon Dam.

Going S from Gortynía via Ellinikó, you will arrive in *Megalópoli*. From here it is easy to visit *Liontári*, a district of considerable archaeological interest. If you then go E, you come to the historic monastery of *Kaltezá*, and eventually to Tegéa, where there are a wealth of archaeological remains and an archaeological museum.

The traveller should not overlook the Kynouría district, where there is much to be seen. The town of Ástros is important because it was here that the foundations of the modern Greek state were laid, when the revolutionary *Constitution of Astros* was drafted. A visit to the local archaeological museum and the nearby *Castle* is well worthwhile. Then there are the village of *Dolianá* and the charming town of Leonídi, which – like nearly all the towns and villages along the coast in this area – is crowded with visitors during the summer season. Of the many traditional settlements to be found further inland, we would strongly recommend a visit to Plátanos, Prastós, Ághios Vasílios, Palaiohóri, and Kosmás.

THESSALY

PREFECTURE OF MAGNISÍA

The prefecture of Magnisía (classical Magnesia) comprises the SW part of mainland Thessaly, plus a long chain of islands known as the Northern Sporades (or just 'the Sporádes') and consisting of Skiáthos, Skópelos, Alónnisos, and sundry smaller islands and islets.

The distinctive geographical feature of the mainland part of the prefecture is the large dog-leg peninsula of Pílio. This closes off the equally large Gulf of Vólos (the Pagasítikos Kólpos), except for the exit from the gulf via the Trikéri strait.

Some 70% of the prefecture is mountain or upland. The principal areas of plain are to the N, as an extension of the Great Plain of Lárisa, or in the C area around Almirós. The highest massifs are Óthrys (1726 m), on the border with Fthiótida, and Pílio (1548 m), the classical *Pelion*, on the peninsula of the same name. There are other high peaks: to the SW, the Goúra range; to the W, Halkodónio;

Volos. This is one of Greece's largest cities. Lying in the nook of the Gulf of Pagasae, it is a good base for touring the prefecture's wonderful mountain scenery and the nearby islands of the Northern Sporades.

Makrinitsa, the main street. This picturesque and historic village lies just north of Volos. There is a good Folk Museum.

and to the N, Mavrovoúni. The prefecture has no large rivers. Nor has it any lakes, for lake Kárla (classical Boibēïs) in the N dried up when a drainage tunnel was opened to take its waters out to sea. The climate of Magnisía is by and large mild and Mediterranean, with the standard fluctuations in temperature between mountain and coast.

Land communication with the prefecture is by road or by rail. There is also considerable sea traffic, mostly freight, to and from the harbour of Vólos. Steamers run to the islands of the Sporádes, and this traffic is heavy during the summer tourist season. The internal road network is mostly adequate, and considerable improvements have been made in the area of Pílio, where there is much tourism. And we must not of course omit to mention one very popular local attraction, the *trenáki* – the narrow-gauge *Pelion Mountain Railway* that takes you from Vólos up to the village of Miliés. This train, whose nickname is *Moutzoúris*, 'Old Smutty', is a national listed monument!

The prefectural capital is Vólos, one of the country's larger urban centres, 317 km from Athens and 219 km from Thessaloníki. This city is in the crook at the N end of the Gulf of Volos. Its population, if we include neighbouring Néa Ionía in the urban complex as a whole, is approximately 120,000. It is an important industrial centre and commercial and fishing port. As you walk along its promenade, you will see the attractive *Papastrátou Building*, and the bridge

from the quay to one arm of the harbour, not far from a *war memorial* to the fallen of the War of Independence. Among buildings of interest in the city are the church of *St Constantine's* (1935); the *Music School* (1882); the *Town Hall*, designed by the leading Greek architect *Pikiónis*; and the *Railway Station* (1884). The *Archaeological Museum*, housed in a neoclassical building of 1907, should on no account be missed: it contains finds from all over Thessaly.

Vólos is at the centre of a region of immense interest to the tourist. Some 5 km to the W is *Dimíni*, where Mycenean *'beehive' tombs* have been brought to light. At the archaeological site of *Sésklos*, one and a half km from the village of the same name, there are the remains of a prehistoric settlement. Continuing further W, you reach the place that is today called Velestíno, 18 km from Vólos. As classical and later *Pherai*, it played a considerable part in Greek history. It was, in particular, the birthplace of *Rígas Feraíos* (= Rhigas of Pherai), one of the architects of Greek revolutionary freedom and a great Balkan political philosopher. The archaeological site here, one of major importance, includes a 4th-c. BC *acropolis*, the *Hyperia fountain*, and a 4th-c. BC Doric *temple of Zeus Thaulios*.

SW of Vólos is the archaeological site of *Demetrias*. Here the major monuments are the *ramparts*, tomb *stelae*, a 3rd-c. BC *theatre*, a *hero shrine*, a 2nd-c. BC *palace*, an *aqueduct*, and the adjacent clas-

Koukounaries, on the island of Skiathos. This famous pine-shaded beach is one of the gems of the Northern Sporades.

Stafylos, a beautiful setting on the island of Skopelos. Skopelos, the classical Peparethus, is an environmentally protected area, with lush green, a wealth of land and marine fauna, and Byzantine monuments.

sical city of *Pagasai*. If you continue SW, after 17.5 km, on the coast, you reach *Néa Anhíalos*, where there are the Late Roman and important Early Christian monuments of classical *Thebes-in-Phthiotis*. Thence on to the township of Almirós, where you should visit the *Archaeological Museum*; the *library of the Classical Society*; the ruins of the ancient city of Hálos (mentioned in Homer); the historic monastery of *Panagía Xeniá*; and the pleasant oakwoods in which are a zoo and a recreation area.

Going N from Vólos, you reach Makrinítsa, a conservation village with vernacular houses, from where there is a superb view across the Gulf of Volos; *Anakasiá*, which has a museum with works by the famous naïve artist *Theófilos*; Portariá, with its stone mansions and cobblestone square; Horeftó; Ta Hánia (1190 m above sea level); and *Moúresi*, with the magnificent beach of Damoúhari.

Going E from Vólos, you reach the mountain district of Pílio and its peninsula. This is certainly the most popular tourist destination for visitors to the prefecture. Not only does it have breathtakingly beautiful countryside; there are many picturesque villages each with its long history, full of buildings in the local style of architecture. There is a *ski centre*, and the *beaches* are simply wonderful. On Pílio, be sure to see *Zagorá*, where Rígas Feraíos went to school; *Tsangaráda*, with the *Nanópoulos School* and the delightful beach of *Fakístra* just nearby; the delightful village of Miliés, where the Thessalian revolutionary *Ánthimos Gazí* was educated at a school that was effectively a university; and *Argalastí*, with the *Hellenic School* at which the educator Delmoúzos and the poet Várnalis both taught. And there are many other places to visit: Anílio, for instance, or Áfyssos, or Vyzítsa, or Kissós. Right in the S of the peninsula there is the charming village of *Trikéri*, 78 km from Vólos. It was one of the leading players in the War of Independence, and is nowadays a sought-after seaside resort.

Crossing the strait from the mainland, the first island you come to in the Sporádes group is Skiáthos. This green and pleasant isle was home to the famous novelist *Papadiamántis* and the local writer Moraïtídis. Its capital and main port has the same name as the island, and is a picturesque little town. The many things to be seen on Skiáthos include its 14th-c. *Castle*; the seaside hamlet of *Koukounar-*

iés ('the umbrella pines'), with its golden sands (*Hrysí Ámmos*) and the adjacent freshwater lagoon of Strofyliá, a conservation area of wetland; and the historic monastery of the *Evangelístria*, begun in 1794 and completed in 1806. The island has many fine beaches: for instance Asélinos, Tzaneriá, Kanapítsa, Vasiliá, Koliós, Vromólimnos, Megáli Ámmos, Fteliá, and 'Banana Beach'.

If you then go E from Skiáthos, the next island you arrive at is Skópelos (classical Peparêthos). This is an environmental conservation area. It has large stretches of *pine forest*, and a wealth of land and sea fauna. It also has 360 churches, from large to tiny: to name but a few, the 18th-c. *Panagía Phaneroméni* and the 17th-c. *Panagía Papameletíou*, the 11th-c. *Episkopí*, and the Byzantine monastery of the *Evangelístria Daponte*. In the island's capital and main port of *Hóra* (or Skópelos) there are vernacular three-storey houses and little narrow alleys to browse in. The island has many beautiful beaches to enjoy your holiday on: Stáfylos, Miliá tou Panórmou, Perivóli, Ai-yiánni, Linarákia.

E of Skópelos there is the extensive Marine Park of the Sporádes. This park enjoys protection under international agreements, and it is here that the remainder of the islands and islets of the Sporádes are mostly to be found – Alónnisos, Kyra-Panagiá, Gioúra, Peristéra, Skántzoura, and so on. The park is home to a rare mammal, the Mediterranean seal (*Monachus monachus*) as well as to various other types of sea and land fauna and flora.

Alónnisos, which etymologically means 'island in the briny', is a favourite hideaway for the discerning visitor. It has an abundance of natural beauty and an ever-changing landscape. Here you can enjoy a quiet holiday, interesting walks, and sea excursions. *Hóra* is built on the site of a medieval castle and has cobbled alleys and whitewashed stone houses. The main town, *Patitíri* (pop. 1700) is also the island's port. Beaches include Fáros, Plakés, Mourtítsa, Megáli Ámmos, Kalyvia, Miliá, Kokkinókastro, and Glyfá. From Alónnisos you can also cross to the small islands to the S and SE (Léhousa, Peristéra, Adelfópoulo, Skatzoúra, and so on). Or you can continue your voyage to the NE, in which case you will reach Kyra-Panagiá and Gioúra. On Gioúra there is a great sea-cave known as the *Cavern of the Cyclops* (Spiliá tou Kyklopa).

The church of Agioi Anargyroi, on the green island of Alonnisos. Here the beauties of nature are enhanced by environmental interest, in the form of a marine park with basking seals, and villages that charm with their traditional architecture.

PREFECTURE OF LÁRISA

The prefecture of Lárisa comprises the W and NW districts of Thessaly, whose largest prefecture it is, both in terms of area and of population. It is washed by the Aegean, to the W. The prefecture has a high percentage (very nearly 50%) of plains. Its main relief feature, lying in the S, is the *Great Plain of Lárisa*. To the W, this extends towards the pref. of Kardítsa, and to the north, towards the pref. of Magnisía.

The loftiest massif in the prefecture, and indeed in the whole of Greece, is *High Olympus* – in Greek, Ólymbos. This is strictly a massif, with its main peak at Mítikas (2917 m), also known as 'the Pantheon'. Olympus is the northernmost physical boundary in the direction of Pieria. The line of mountains continues to the S, with Low Olympus (Káto Ólymbos), *Kíssavos* (classical Óssa), and Megavoúni. To the east of Olympus proper is the height of Títaros. Continuing along the prefecture's W boundaries, we find mts Kamvoúni, Antihásia, Zárkos, and Dobroútsi (classical Títanos). Right in the S of the prefecture, straddling the border with Fthiótida, is mt Nathráki.

The core of the prefecture's hydrography is the r. *Piniós*. This enters the prefecture from the W, between mt Zárkos and mt

Larisa. This city is one of the busiest places in Greece.

Dobroútsi. It then follows an E to NE course. Having passed through the Vale of Tempe (Témbi), between mt Káto Ólymbos and mt Kíssavos, it empties into the Aegean, in the S of the Gulf of Thérmi. Its principal affluents are, to the S, the Enipéas, and in the N central part, the Titarísios. The climate of the prefecture shows great variations, depending on the terrain. It tends to be of the Continental type, with extreme fluctuations of temperature as between summer and winter.

Communication with the prefecture of Lárisa is basically by road (the Athens-Lárisa motorway) or by rail.

The prefectural capital is the city of Lárisa, which is one of the country's larger urban centres (pop. approx. 125,000). The city lies a little to the W of centre in the prefecture, on the banks of the r. Piniós, 351 km from Athens and 155 km from Thessaloníki. Historically, Lárisa is the oldest city in Greece, for it has been inhabited ever since the Palaeolithic Age. It was here that *Hippocrates*, 'the Father of Medicine', lived, and died (in 377 BC). Over the course of the centuries, it has endured one foreign ruler after another, but has always played a leading part in the historical fortunes of Thessaly. The remains of the ancient *acropolis* are extant. There are two ancient *theatres*, and major Christian *churches* and monuments. Today Lárisa is a hive of cultural activity, a lively place where of an evening you can enjoy an ouzo and mezé in one of its spacious *squares*. The exhibits in the *Archaeological Museum* date from the Neolithic Age through to Byzantine times. The *Folk Museum* acts as a focus for major cultural events. Also rewarding to visit are the city's *Art Gallery* and its large and pleasant park, the *Alcazar*.

Elsewhere in the prefecture, too, there are towns well worth the journey. Tírnavos is a place with a long history, though perhaps best known today for the excellent ouzo which it produces. Fársala (classical Pharsalus, where *Julius Caesar* won his greatest victory) is today a centre of commerce (cotton, fudgemaking) but has a history going back to Neolithic times (its 'beehive' tomb). Near *Elassóna* is the historic *Olymbiótissa* monastery, founded by the Byzantine emperor Andronicus II Palaeologus. Near Agiá, in the district called *Nerómili* ('Watermills'), is a famous *Roman Baths*. Agiókambos is a seaside village with a superb *long sandy beach* running as far as the neighbouring villages of Sotirítsa and Velíka. Perhaps the jewel of the prefecture for the tourist is the historic village of Ambelákia, perched on mount Kíssavos, with its handful of fine vernacular buildings. It was here, at the turn of the 18th century, that the very first *cooperative* in Greece (and perhaps in the world) was set up, to enjoy great success. The village's showpiece is the *Mansion of George Schwartz* (the cooperative's president), a three-storeyed building (which is exceptional) with wonderful rococo painted interiors

←

The Vale of Tempe. Long recognized as a place of incomparable beauty, Tempe is the tree-shaded valley of the river Peneius, running between mount Olympus and mount Ossa to debouch into the Aegean Sea.

and carved woodwork. A drive through landscape of rare beauty brings you to *Karítsa*, on the slopes of mount Kíssavos, 55 km NE of the capital, and thence to *Kókkino Neró* and a large number of other beautiful beaches.

The prefecture of Lárisa also lends itself to *climbing expeditions*. Usually the route is via the mountain refuges, and the final objective is to scale the peak of *Mytikas*, the apex of Greece, the place where the Olympian gods were traditionally believed (and still are, locally) to have their home. 'Low Olympus', Kíssavos, and Títaros are all regions well worth exploring, as is *Tsaritsáni*, a large and historic village with numerous attractions. Of the beauty of the *Vale of Tempe* – formed by the lower reaches of the river Piniós, and one of the loveliest of all Greek landscapes – many travellers, ancient and modern, have written lyrical accounts. It seems a pity that so many drivers should regard this sublime valley as merely a convenient point at which to stop for a sandwich, rather than as a place of interest for the visitor.

Ambelakia. It was in this picturesque little place, now a conservation area, at the foot of mount Ossa, that the first known Cooperative flourished on Greek soil in the 18th and 19th centuries.

PREFECTURE OF TRÍKALA

The prefecture of Tríkala (also Tríkkala) comprises the NW districts of Thessaly, and has no outlet to the sea. It is largely (approximately 85%) mountain or upland. The one extensive area of plain is in the SE, and is a continuation of the Great Plain of Thessaly, most of which lies in the pref. of Lárisa. Broadly speaking, the W terrain of the prefecture forms part of the south Píndos system. The major peaks on the border with the pref. of Yánnina include the Athamaniká mountains, with their peak of Tzoumérka (2469 m); Lákmos; and the Áspra Lithária heights. To the N of the latter is the *Stenó tis Katáras*, 'the Defile of the Curse', the way through from Thessaly to Epirus. The principal massifs to the N are the 'twins' Hásia and Antihásia, towards the prefs. of Grevená and Lárisa. To the E are the somewhat lower mountains of Zárkos and Títanos, with the river Piniós flowing down the valley between them. In the interior of the prefecture, too, there are still further high peaks, such as Tringía or mt Kerkéti (also known as Kótziakas).

Meteora, near Kalambaka. On the tops of these lofty limestone pillars, unique in Europe for their geological formation, there still dwells a historic community of monks. Kalambaka itself has substantial tourist facilities, a conference centre, and a school of woodcarving.

The main feature of the prefecture's hydrography is its three rivers. The first is the r. Ahelóös, which runs S in the W districts and on which are the man-made lakes of Mesohóra and Sykiá, the second of these forming a boundary with the pref. of Árta. The second is the r. Piniós, which flows towards the pref. of Lárisa. The third is the r. Lithaíos (also known as the Trikalinós), which joins the Piniós at Tríkala. Generally speaking, the local climate is of the Continental type, with variations of temperature, rainfall and snowfall depending on terrain.

Communications with the prefecture of Tríkala are by road and by rail (though the line goes only as far as Kalambáka). The local road network is in a satisfactory state.

The capital is the town of Tríkala (pop. approx. 50,000). This lies in the SW plain, 331 km from Athens and 216 km from Thessaloníki. The modern town is built on the site of the classical city of *Tricce*, traditionally the birthplace of *Asclepius*, the Greek god of medicine. Of the many things to see in Tríkala your first visit should perhaps be to the nearby archaeological site, with its *Asclepium*, a 'treatment centre' of which you can still the remains (these include part of a Late Hellenistic building, with a Roman mosaic floor); part of a Late Hellenistic *stoa*; and part of a *Roman Baths*. Then there are the town's Byzantine *fort*, built by the emperor Justinian; and its 16th- and 17th century churches (*St John the Baptist, St John the Charitable, St Demetrius, Agía Paraskeví*). Other public buildings include the *Dorothea School* (1875), a handsome stone edifice; the *bridge* in

View of Trikala. The modern town has usurped the site and the name of the classical city of Trikka, traditionally the birth place of Asclepius, god of healing.

Meteora, the Monastery of the Holy Trinity. As can be seen, this 15th-century monastery is far from easy to get to.

the centre of town over the river Lithaíos (1886); a *folk museum*; the *Public Library*; and the *Art Gallery*.

To the N of Tríkala is the *Cavern of Theópetra*. Here were found objects ranging in date from the Middle Palaeolithic to the Neolithic Age. A little further in the same direction is the historic township of Kalambáka, with the historic church of the *Dormition* (10th or 11th c). The town has, by the way, ample hotel accommodation, a state-of-the-art *conference centre*, and Greece's one and only *college of woodcarving*.

You then come to Metéora (the name means 'in mid-air'). This world-famous monastic community is the largest in Greece excepting that of Mount Athos, while Metéora's towering *pinnacles of grey rock* are a geological phenomenon unparalleled in Europe. The monasteries to see are: *Megálou Meteórou* (14th c.), the Great Metéoron, which has a katholikon (principal place of worship) dedicated to the *Transfiguration*, and has also a museum; *Barlaám* (16th c.), with its katholikon dedicated to *All Saints* and side-chapel of the Three Hierarchs; *Rousánou* (16th c.), dedicated to the *Transfiguration* and to St Barbara; *Agíou Nikoláou Anapafsá* (16th c.), where the frescoes in the katholikon are the work of the great ecclesiastical painter Theodore *Strelítzas*, from Crete; *Agíou Stefánou* (16th c. – the katholikon, which is dedicated to the martyr Charalambos, is later); and *Agías Triádos* (15th c.), not an easy place to get to, with its 130 steps.

The prefecture has many other monuments, historical and ecclesiastical: for instance the prehistoric settlement at *Platiá Magoúla*, in the Zárkos mountains E of Tríkala, near the border with the pref. of Lárisa; or W of Tríkala, near the border with the pref. of Kardítsa, the *Megálon Pylón* ('Great Gate') monastery, built by the Byzantine dignitary John Angelos Doúkas Komninós in 1283.

The hill villages of this prefecture are numerous and picturesque. Built among fir woods, they are specially suited to winter tourism. We would recommend *Pertoúli*, 1150 m above sea level, at 48 km (all distances are from Tríkala); *Kastaniá*, 500 m above sea level, in the Aspropótamos area, at 56 km; *Neraïdohóri*, 'village of the water fairies', 1140 m above sea level, at 59 km; and *Eláti*, 860 m above sea level, at 34 km.

PREFECTURE OF KARDÍTSA

The prefecture of Kardítsa comprises the SW districts of Thessaly and has no outlet to the sea. There is a zone of mountain and upland in the S and W, covering just over half (54%) of the prefecture. The terrain then runs down towards the broad plains of the C and NE that form the western extension of the Great Plain of Thessaly and cover the remainder (46%) of the prefecture. The mountainous part of Kardítsa belongs to the south Píndos and Ágrafa system. Its highest peaks are Karáva (2184 m), in the hinterland to the W, and Delemídi (2163 m) and Voutsikáki (2154 m) on the border with Evritanía.

The prefecture has an unusually rich system of rivers, lakes and springs. It includes the two great waterways of the r. Ahelóös and the r. Piniós, which separate it from the prefs. of Árta and Tríkala respectively. There is a host of other smaller rivers in the hinterland (for instance the Pámisos, the Enipéas, the Apidanós and the Sofiadítikos). There are also Kardítsa's four great man-made lakes: Límni Smokóvou, in the SE, towards Fthiótida; Límni Plastíra, in the W central part; Límni Mouzakíou, in the N, towards Tríkala; and Límni Sykiás, in the W, towards the prefs. of Tríkala or Árta. The climate is by and large of the Continental type, with divergences between the mountain and the plain.

Karditsa, the Square.

Communication with the prefecture is by road, or by rail (in which case you have to change on to the branch line at Fársala). There is a reasonably comprehensive internal road network, especially in the plains.

The prefecture's capital and its only town of any size is Kardítsa (pop. approx. 32,000). It lies in the C of the prefecture, on the W edge of the Great Plain of Thessaly, 301 km from Athens. Kardítsa was founded during the Turkish period, but its real development, as the *agricultural and industrial hub* of western Thessaly, began only when it became part of Greece in 1881.

As you stroll round the town you will see the main sights it has to offer: the cathedral church of *St Constantine's* and the church of *Zoödohou Pigís*, both 19th-c.; the early 20th-c. *Public Market*; the pleasant and extensive *Pafsílipo Park*; the *Folk Museum*, with its collection of memorabilia concerning General *Plastíras*, prime mover of the revolution of 1922; and the nearby *Fanári Fort*, NE of the town centre.

The N part of the prefecture is exceptionally rewarding for the nature-lover. There is a scenic route including *Límni Smokóvou*, where you may want to 'take the waters' at the *spa bath*, via *Redína* (the 'Queen of the Ágrafa Mountains'), through to Límni Plastíra, with its very beautiful lakeland scenery. Created in 1959, by closing off the lake of Mégdova with the Tavropós barrage, this has gradually evolved into one of central Greece's main biotopes. The Límni Plastíra area is a good base from which to explore the many picturesque villages in the district (for instance Filaktí, Niohóri, *Neráïda*, Pezoúla, and Krionéri), and the historic monastery of *Koróni*, founded by the Komninós (Comnene) dynasty in the 12th century.

Moving onwards, you reach *Argithéa*, at the extreme W end of the prefecture, boxed in by three other prefs. (Tríkala, Árta, Evritanía). This is a region rich in history and geography. Connected with the very early historical presence of the Athamánes, it is today a good area for 'green tourism'. Places to visit include the *banks of the river Ahelóös* and the small but pretty villages, such as Anthiró, Argithéa itself, Elliniká, or Therinó. Also well worth discovering are the area's historic cave churches and monasteries – *Spiliá, Metamórphosi tou Sotíros* (the Transfiguration), *Ágias Triádas* (the Trinity), *Genníseos Theotókou* (the Virgin Mary).

After Argithéa there are two options. One is to return to Kardítsa via the *Mouzáki* district and its man-made lake, also a favoured spot for nature-lovers, and the central plain of the prefecture with its lush river landscapes. The other is to spend some time visiting the many settlements of importance in the area, in particular *Palamás* and *Sofádes*.

View of Lake Plastira.
This manmade lake in the
Karditsa prefecture was created
in 1959 by damming the river
Megdovas. Over the years it has
become one of the major
biotopes in central Greece.

EPIRUS

PREFECTURE OF THESPROTÍA

The prefecture of Thesprotía comprises the NW part of Epirus (Ípiros), and hence of mainland Greece. Its N boundaries also form part of the frontier between Greece and Albania. To the S and W, it is washed by the Ionian Sea. It is by and large upland or mountain, though it does also have areas of coastal and river plain. In terms of terrain it belongs to the northern Píndos in general. The principal massifs are mt Tsamantá (1806 m), also known as Mourgána, on the Greek-Albanian border; the roughly parallel ranges of Paramythiá and Soúli, to the E, towards the pref. of Yánnina; the Filiátes range in the hinterland to the NW; and the low range of hills behind Párga, to the SW, towards the pref. of Préveza.

The basis of the prefecture's hydrography is the river Kalamás (the classical Thyamis), which empties north of Igoumenítsa, plus the Kokytós-Ahéron river system, which later enters the pref. of Préveza, to empty south of Párga. The coastal strip is fairly heavily indented, with bays at Sagiáda, Igoumenítsa, Platariás and elsewhere. All along it there are a number of islets, such as Ágios Nikólaos. The climate is variable, depending on the terrain: it is relatively mild in the plains and on the coast, but harsher in the mountain areas of the interior.

Communications with the prefecture are by road and by sea. Igoumenítsa is a large harbour for commercial freight and passenger vessels.

The prefecture's capital, and its main urban centre, is Igoumenítsa (pop. approx. 9000). It lies in the bend of the Gulf of Igoumenítsa, 480 km from Athens. After being reduced to a shell by the Germans in the Second World War, it made a gradual recovery, to become a major commercial and tourist centre. Igoumenítsa's principal historical sites are the Turkish *Castle*, slighted by Morosini in 1685; the *Cultural Centre*; and the *County Hall*.

The town is a good base from which to explore the locality, whether along the coast or inland. If you go N, you reach (after 3 km) Pírgos-in-Rágio, a Late Archaic *fort* designed to protect Corcyra's colony of *Peraía*; then ancient *Gitáni*, seat of the Thesprotian, and for a time of the Epirot, commonwealth. You can also explore the lower reaches of the Kalamás and the remarkable wetlands of its delta, before going down to the superb beaches of Sagiáda Bay. Or by striking into the interior you can reach historic *Filiátes*, and continue from there to the verdant slopes of hills such as mt

Sibota. This historic district south of Igoumenitsa has numerous good beaches and a wealth of natural beauty. It is a popular summer resort.

The bay and harbour of Sagiada (with Makronoros in the distance). It was here that the main estuary of the river Kalamas (the classical Thyamis) once lay.

View of Igoumenitsa.
This town, capital of the prefec-
ture of Thesprotia, has a major
freight and passenger port.
It is also an important tourist
destination, with an impressive
castle that was badly knocked
about by the Venetian admiral
Morosini in 1685.

Mourgána, with their diverse natural beauty.

S of the capital there are excellent long beaches. We would specially recommend the tourist village of *Platariás*, 12 km from Igoumenítsa; historic *Síbota*, with its perfect shores; and the stretch of coast from Pérdika, 37 km from Igoumenítsa, all the way down to Párga in the pref. of Préveza.

If you are touring the hinterland you should certainly make a visit to the township of Paramythiá, with its 13th c. church of *Megáli Panagía* and its *Castle of St Donatus*; to the archaeological site at *Eléa*; to historic Margaritári with its 16th c. fort, its minaret, and its immemorial plane trees; to the banks of the rivers *Kokytós* and *Ahéron*, with their rich landscape and wealth of mythical associations; and the ruins of a Byzantine *basilica* at Glikí, a village in a very charming natural setting, with cool fresh running water. If you like mountain tourism, you would do well to find your way up on to the parallel ranges of Paramythiá and Soúli. Finally, there is a history excursion to the villages of the *Valley of Soúli* in the SE of the prefecture, in between the two mountains just mentioned: Avlótopos, Tsangári, Koukoulií, Frosyni and their neighbours. All these played a heroic part in the long-drawn struggle to wrest freedom from their Ottoman rules, and all paid a heavy price in blood.

PREFECTURE OF IOANNINA

The prefecture of Yánnina (officially Ioánnina) comprises the NE districts of Epirus (Ípiros), and has no outlet to the sea. Its NW border forms part of the frontier between Greece and Albania. Nearly the whole of the prefecture is mountain or upland, and belongs to the terrain of the Pindus range in general. Its highest massifs are in the N: Smólikas (2637 m); *Grámmos* (2520 m) on the border with the pref. of Kastoriá and the frontier with Albania; Tymfi (2497 m). To the E, towards the pref. of Tríkala, is the peak Lákmos. To the S are, towards the prefs. of Tríkala and Árta, the peak Tzoumérka and the Athamaniká range; towards the prefs. of Árta and Préveza, the peak of Xerovoúni; and towards the pref. of Thesprotía, the *mountains of Soúli*. To the W are Tómaros and Kasidiáris. In the C part of the prefecture is mt *Mitsikéli*.

The most substantial area of flat land is around Yánnina itself, between mts Mitsikéli and Tómaros. The system of rivers, lakes and springs is fairly complex. It comprises four main waterways, the r. Aóös, the r. Árakhthos, the r. Loúros, and the r. Thyamis (also known as the Kalamás), together with their affluents. There are two princi-

The lake isle of Ioannina. This inhabited island lies right in the middle of lake Pambotis. It is well worth visiting for – amongst other things – the summer house of the tyrant Ali Pasha, and two historic monasteries (St Nicholas and St Panteleimon).

pal lakes, the Lake of Yánnina (officially Pamvótis) and the man-made reservoir on the Aóös, to the E. The climate follows the terrain and shows great variations: by and large it is of Continental type, and the winters are notably severe.

Communication with the prefecture is by road and by air. Plans are under way for rail links with Athens and Thessaloniki.

The prefectural capital and principal town is Yánnina (Ioánnina) (pop. approx. 62,000). It lies in the Plain of Yánnina, 445 km from Athens and 370 km from Thessaloníki. There are several, and conflicting, theories about Yánnina's historical origins. The first written records that clearly refer to the town date only from the Middle Byzantine period. In the centuries following it was occupied by many conquerors from various countries. It enjoyed an early period of prosperity in the 13th century. In 1431 it fell to the Ottoman Turks, who granted the city privileged status. Its last great days were from 1788 to 1820, as the chosen seat of the autocrat *Ali Paşa*, after which it fell into comparative obscurity. It was not liberated until February 1913, after the fall of Bizáni. From then on, it proved itself the most important urban centre in the whole of Epirus. It became the seat of a *university* and various other learned bodies. Today it has a thriving cultural identity, an atmosphere of its own, and a busy night life.

The major historical attraction for the visitor to Yánnina must surely be its fortress, the Froúrio, whose many eye-catching build-

Papingo, north east of Ioannina. This very picturesque place lies in the shadow of the Tymfi mountain range. Over the past few years it has become a favourite destination for summer as well as winter holidays.

Yannina, the Castle. In the neighbourhood of the Castle there are many impressive buildings constructed in the traditional style of Epirus. Within the castle walls there are two mosques: one of these (the Aslan-pasha mosque) now houses the Civic Museum, with interesting exhibits which include the sword of the Greek Revolutionary general Karaiskakis.

View of Metsovo. There is much to see in this charming town rich in traditional architecture, including the Tositsa Mansion, with an exhibition of folk art, and the cathedral church of Agia Paraskevi.

ings, built in the distinctive Epirot style, still cluster within and outside its perimeter walls. Inside the fortress, there are two mosques, one of which, the *Cami of Aslan Paşa*, now houses the *Municipal Museum*, one exhibit being the sword of admiral *Karaïskákis*. Other worthwhile places to visit are the excellent *Archaeological Museum*; the *Folk Art Collection*; the *Society of Epirot Studies* with its gallery of historical paintings; and the city's two largest book collectiosn, the *Zosimaia Library* and the *Library of the Society of Epirot Studies*). The *Vrelli Museum* has a quaint collection of waxworks. The *Cave of Perama* is a short drive from the town. For a truly memorable experience, you should take a boat trip on the beautiful Lake of Yánnina, crossing to the small inhabited island in the middle, a delightful spot with two famous monasteries, *St Nicholas* and *St Panteleimon*, as well as the very room in which Ali Paşa was finally cornered by his enemies.

SSE of Yánnina is Ancient Dodóna, home of the second most important classical Greek oracle after Delphi. The principal attractions on the archaeological site are the great *theatre*, dating from the reign of king Pyrrhus in the 3rd c. BC; the ruins of a *temple of Zeus*; a *council chamber* of the 4th or 3rd c. BC; a 3rd-c. *stadium*; the 4th-c. *acropolis*; and the 4th-c. *prytaneum* which was in all probability the residence of the priests of Zeus. N of Yánnina, and also of great interest to the student of antiquity, are two other archaeological sites: one at *Rodotópi*, with a shrine of the Molossians' local deity *Zeus Áreios*; the other at *Ágios Minás*, with excavations are still in progress, and where there have been important finds from the Palaeolithic Age.

One very pleasant excursion from Yánnina is through the mountainous E part of the prefecture. The highlight of this trip is the charming and historic town of Métsovo, with its traditional buildings in the Epirot style. Its various attractions include the *Tosítsas Mansion*, which houses a museum of folk art; the 15th-c. metropolitan church of *Agía Paraskeví*; the 17th-c. monastery of *St Nicholas*; the *Art Gallery*; the 17th-c. *Panagía* monastery; and 18th- and 19th-c. *fountains* in the vernacular style. Métsovo is also a good base from which to visit the three *ski centres* of the Pindos range (at Karakóli, Prophítis Ilías and Zygós), or to explore the surrounding countryside, starting with the huge artificial dam on the river Aóös and then wandering through the extensive forests (approx. 17,000 acres) of the Valia Kálda National Park – a place to lose oneself in, and a conservation area. The Park, which spills over into the neighbouring pref. of Grevená, is home to a rare variety of fauna, including roedeer, bear, otters, wildcats, and birds of prey. It has alternating stretches of forest and greensward.

Another unforgettable experience is the excursion to the Zagorohória, the scatter of villages, each steeped in history, across the High Zagóri, N of Yánnina between mt Mitsikéli and mt Tymfi. This is another conservation area of rare natural beauty. It contains one of the richest ecosystems in the Balkans. The villages, of which there many, reached an economic and intellectual peak in the days of Ottoman rule, and were rewarded with self-governing status. To name but a few of them: *Vovoúsa* (1000 m above sea level) with its humpback stone bridge dating from 1748; *Vítsa* (960 m); *Dílofo* (880

An enchanting landscape in the Vikos-Voidomatis area, one of many that will delight the lover of nature. 'Green tourism' is on the rise in Greece.

The awesome Vikos Gorge. The river Vikos (also known as Voidomatis) runs down a canyon some 12 miles long, with an average depth of over two and a half thousand feet. Not only is this a spectacular rock formation; it is also part of a region with tremendous interest to the ecologist. Here forest fauna and flora are in abundance, with numerous rare species of birds and mammals.

Dodona, the large ancient theatre. At Dodona there was an oracle which the classical Greek world regarded as second in importance only to Delphi itself.

m) with its mansions of stone; *Díkorfo*, with its vernacular Epirot houses and bridges; Miliotádes; *Dóliani*; Greveníti, where there is a trout farm; Arísti, with the 16th-c. monastery of the *Panagía Spiliótissa* (Our Lady of the Cavern); *Víkos*, famous for its *gorge*, with the adjacent *Víkos & Aöös National Park*; the picturesque cobble-stones of *Monodéndri* (1060 m); Elafótopos (1100 m); Upper and Lower Pedinó; *Pápingo*, a charming settlement dating from the 14th century; Kípi, where there is a *folk museum*; Koukoúli & Laísta; Skam-néli; Negádes; and *Chepélovo* (1080 m), whose bridges, churches, and art gallery attract large numbers of visitors every year.

Going directly N from the Zagorohória, you soon arrive at Kónitsa. This township was founded in Byzantine times. Its most flourishing period was in the reign of Alí Paşa. There is much to see, including impressive *mansion houses*, *churches*, and a *museum of folk-lore*. Kónitsa is steadily being developed for tourism.

Last but not least, there is the 'far west' of the prefecture, and this too is well worth visiting. You will certainly want to stop in such attractive villages and towns as Kefalóvryso, *Pogonianí*, *Delvináki*, Dolianá, Lavdáni, Byron's Zítsa with its *monastery*, Zálongo, and Petoúsi.

PREFECTURE OF ÁRTA

The prefecture of Árta comprises the SE part of Epirus (Ípiros). It is washed by the Ambracian Gulf, a closed bay, to the S. Approximately three quarters of the prefecture, chiefly its N and E districts, is mountain or upland. The principal massifs are the Athamaniká range, with the peak of *Tzoumérka* (2393 m), to the north; the end of the Váltos range, to the SE; and mt Kokkinólakkos, to the E. To the SW is the broad alluvial Ambracian Plain (also known as the Plain of Árta). The coastline is in general flat, with extensive indentations – for instance, the lagoons of Rodiá and Logaroú – along which are low-lying islets. The prefecture's hydrography is fairly rich: its basic elements are, to the W, the r. Árahthos and the great man-made barrage lake of Árahthos; and to the E, the river Ahelóös, with the man-made Lake of Sykiá, on the border with the prefs. of Tríkala and Kardítsa. The climate is variable, depending on the terrain: in the plains and on the coast it is relatively mild, and in the mountains of the interior, harsher.

Communication with the prefecture is by road; normally via the Athens-Patras motorway, and then across the *new suspension bridge* from Río to Antírrio. A slower route is the cross-country through road from Athens via Livadiá, Delphi, Náfpaktos, Mesolónghi, and Amfilohía.

Arta, the Byzantine castle. This well preserved structure is recorded from as early as the 9th century; the major part of it is later, dating from the Comnene period. Today it is the home of an open-air municipal theatre.

The Bridge at Arta.
Throughout south eastern
Europe there are variants of the
ballad about this legendary
bridge and the mastermason
who, when building it, walled his
wife up in it 'to make it firm'.

The prefecture's capital, and only sizeable town, is Árta itself (pop. approx. 20,000). This lies in the fertile Ambracian Plain, on the lower reaches of the river Árahthos, 360 km from Athens. Árta was the seat of the *Despotate of Epirus*. Often having to endure foreign occupation, the longest being that of the Ottoman Turks, the town was eventually reunited with Greece only in 1881. Of the many things to see in Árta and its environs, we would recommend the well-preserved Byzantine *Castle*, built by the Komninós (Comnene) dynasty in the 13th century, and now housing an open-air *Municipal Theatre*. From the classical period there are the remains of a Late Archaic *temple of Apollo*, dating from about 500 BC, next to which is Amvrakía's 4th or 3rd century '*little theatre*'; and also some remnants, probably 4th-century, of the town's classical *walls*. Árta's medieval churches are the famous *Panagía Parigorítissa* (13th c.), with a small archaeological and Byzantine *museum*; *St Basil's* (14th c.), *St Mark's* (1770); and *St Theodora's* (13th c.). There are two historic monasteries: the *Káto Panagía* (13th c.), and the *Panagía of Vlachérna*, which contains the tombs of the Komninós dynasty.

And of course there is the Bridge of Árta – that fine piece of craftsmanship, famous in song and story. According to the legend, the masterbuilder, ere finishing the bridge, walled up his wife in it. Sombre memories, too, are attached to the Great Plane Tree of Arta nearby, for from its branches the Ottomans hanged unruly Greeks in the days of the Turkish occupation.

Leaving the town of Árta, there are a variety of destinations for the visitor as he or she tours the prefecture. To the S there are such historic places to visit as Pétas, where a famous *battle* took place in 1822 between Greeks and Turks; Kombóti; and Anéza. Or you can explore the countryside of the lower r. Árahthos; the *lagoons*; and the beautiful small island of *Koronisía*. In the central part of the prefecture there is the great dam on the r. Árahthos. From there you can go W, towards Gríbovo, Ammótopos, and the nearby archaeological site of *Orrháos*; or W, towards Upper Kalentíni and Astrohóri. If you go into the N of the prefecture, a mainly mountainous area, you can choose between a large number of picturesque and historic villages, surrounded by wonderful countryside: Athamánio, Vourgaréli, Theodóriana, Ágnanta, and so on. Other visits worth making are to the banks of the Ahelóös and the man-made Lake of Sykiá.

The historic church of Our Lady of Vlacherna, north east of Arta. This three-aisled basilica dates essentially from the 13th century. It was here that members of the ruling family of Epirus, the Comnenes, were buried.

PREFECTURE OF PRÉVEZA

Shaped like an inverted triangle, the prefecture of Préveza comprises the SW part of Epirus (Ípiros). To the W it is washed by the Ionian Sea, to the SE by the Ambracian Gulf, and to the S by the Strait of Préveza and Áktio.

Three quarters of the prefecture is mountain or upland. The main massifs, lying in the NE, are Xerovoúni (1607 m) and the S outcrops of mt Tómaros, with a peak at Zarkoráhi (1332 m). It has a rich hydrographic network. The principal waterways are the r. *Ahéron* (classical Acheron) with its affluents, which empties into the Ionian Sea, and the r. Loúros, which empties into the Ambracian Gulf. Both form broad alluvial plains. The coasts are low-lying and strikingly indented – not only in the S, with harbourages at Salaóra, Préveza itself and Nikópoli, but in the NW, with the harbour of Agíou Ioánni. The climate is variable, depending on the terrain: in the plains and on the coast it is relatively mild, and in the mountains of the interior, harsher.

Preveza. Guarding the mouth of the Ambracian Gulf, and lying on the same site as the classical city of Berenicia, Preveza is a spick-and-span town with many attractive buildings and streets from the historical past.

Communication with the prefecture is by road: normally via the Athens-Patras motorway, and then across the *new suspension bridge* from Río to Antírrio. A slower route is the cross-country through road from Athens via Livadiá, Delphi, Náfpaktos, Mesolónghi, and Agrínio.

Most visitors make their first acquaintance with the prefecture when arriving in its capital, Préveza (pop. approx. 17,000), 430 km from Athens and 440 km from Thessaloníki. The town lies at the mouth of the Ambracian Gulf, on the site of the classical city of *Berenicia*. It has a road link with Áktio, by a tunnel beneath the Strait, and is a port of some importance. Its *mansions* in the traditional style, its cobbled alleys, and its picturesque *promenade* crowded with fashionable waterfront cafes for ouzo and a snack, all lend it a 'Greek island' atmosphere. It has two specialist *museums* – one for the great sea battle of Actium and one for natural history – and three forts, the *Castle of God the Almighty*, the *Castle of St Andrew*, and the *Castle of St George*.

Some 7 km N of Préveza is the extensive archaeological site (2250 acres) of Roman Nicopolis. This was the city founded by Octavianus, later to become Augustus Caesar, after winning the *sea battle of Actium* (31 BC). Nicopolis was besieged and captured time and again, until it was finally abandoned in the ninth or tenth century. The major classical remains on the site are the Roman *walls*; the 1st-c. AD concert-hall

View of Parga. This enchanting and much-visited little town is built in the curve of the hill, on the north west shores of the prefecture of Preveza.

Panoramic view of the course of the Acheron. This river, famous in classical Greek myth, discharges into the Ionian, forming a broad alluvial plain.

(*odeum*), with its rows of seats, pit, and stage; the *North Baths*, a Roman public building; *Augustus Caesar's monument* (29-27 BC), with its dedication to the war gods Mars, Neptune, and Apollo Actius; a *theatre*; and a *shrine of the Nymphs*. The visitor will also want to visit Nicopolis' Byzantine ecclesiastical and other monuments (six *basilicas*, the *Bishop's Palace*, the Byzantine *walls*, a *villa*), and the on-site *archaeological museum*. It may also be of interest that at Píges tou Loúrou (the springs of the river Loúros), a little to the N, there is the Roman *aqueduct* – also provided by Octavianus - that brought water to the city of Nicopolis.

Going N from Nicopolis, you arrive at the archaeological site of *Kassópi*. A flourishing city during the 3rd c. BC, it was destroyed by the Romans in 168 BC. The remains of the *North Stoa*, the *prytaneum*, a *hostel*, and a *dwelling-house* still survive. Further W, at Rízon, is a Roman *villa*. Still this far N, but over in the direction of the pref. of Árta, is the fort of *Rogés* (classical Buchetium, with a citadel and enceinte built on ashlar foundations). Further N, in the vicinity of the Roman aqueduct mentioned in the previous paragraph, you reach *Asproháliko*, where there have been finds from the Palaeolithic age. You should not miss the

chance to visit, at the village of Mesopótamos (41 km from Préveza), the celebrated Oracle of the Dead (Necromanteíon) near the river Ahéron; the village of *Kypséli*; and the sheer drop to the river Ahéron at Zálongo, where in 1803 the women of the village chose to throw themselves dancing over the precipice rather than surrender to Alí Paşa.

Párga, 60 km from Préveza, is one of the prettiest of all Greek towns, with its *Castle*, its sea caves, its islets, and the blue-green waters of the Saracenic Gulf.

Other places to see as you tour the prefecture include *Kanaláki*, with the classical site of Pandosia; *Thesprotikó*, where there is a *women's agricultural cooperative* that produces, amongst other things, *trahanas* and *hylópites* (cereals and pasta, for soups), and traditional candies and sweetmeats; Skepastó; *Filippiáda*, a modern town, and Gorgómylos, both of which are set in very lovely countryside. The pick of the prefecture's coastal villages are Loútsa, Lygiá, Kastrosykiá, Kanáli, and Mytikas, all of which are charming seaside resorts. *Ammoudiá*, at the delta of the Ahéron, is particularly recommended for its superb beach.

View of the archaeological site of Nicopolis. This Roman city founded by Octavian in 31 B.C. shortly after the battle of Actium started to fall apart only in the 10th century. Here is its splendid Odeum (concert hall), complete with stage, and semicircular seating and 'pit'.

Thessaloniki, the Marine Parade,
with (right) the White Tower.
The latter, the city's emblem,
was to be known in Turkish times
as 'the Bloody Tower' (Kanlı Kule).
It had been erected by the Venetians
at the start of the 15th century,
as part of the city's southern
fortifications.

MACEDONIA

PREFECTURE OF THESSALONIKI

The prefecture of Thessaloníki comprises districts of central Macedonia: the N part of the peninsula of Halkidikí, plus the hinterland. It has the second largest population of any Greek prefecture, exceeded only by Attica.

The prefecture is washed by the Gulf of Thessaloníki (the N end of the Gulf of Thérmi), to the W; and by the Gulf of Strimónas, to the E. It is two thirds (about 65%) plainland, with the main plains being those of Thessaloníki and Langadás. The principal massifs are, to the S, Hortiátis (1201 m); to the N, Vertískos (1103 m); and to the east, Kedrílio (1091 m). All these are ideal excursions for lovers of nature.

The prefecture's system of rivers, lakes and streams is a rich one. It comprises the lower reaches of the r. Loudías, the natural

Thessaloniki, Aristotle Square. Much of Thessaloniki's most important economic and social life goes on here, in what is the largest open space in the city precincts,. It is a very pleasant and relaxing place to sit or take a stroll.

Thessaloniki, the Arch of Galerius. Standing in the very centre of the city, 'the Kamára', with its superb Roman reliefs, is a reminder of an emperor's triumphs in battle.

boundary with Imathía, and the rivers Axiós and Gallikós, both of which have done their bit to form the contour of the plain, by silting up. The hydrographic system also includes two large interconnecting lakes, Lake Langadás and Lake Vólvi. Though variable, the climate tends to be Continental, with chilly winters, hot summers, and high rainfall and snowfall.

Communication with the prefecture is by road (the Athens -Thessaloníki - Alexandroúpoli motorway, and other roads), by rail (the main Athens-Thessaloníki-Alexandroúpoli line, with branch lines northwards), and by air. The road network within the prefecture is reasonably extensive and is generally in satisfactory repair.

The city of Thessaloníki (pop. approx. 400,000), the prefecture's capital and largest urban centre, lies in the crook of the Bay of Thessaloníki, 514 km from Athens. It spreads up the slopes of mt Hortiátis and is only a short way from the mouths of the r. Gallikós.

Frequently referred to as 'the co-capital of Greece' or as 'the capital of Macedonia', Thessaloníki is not only the most important economic, administrative, and intellectual centre in northern Greece, but one of the principal cities of the Balkans. It has a *university*, a polytechnic, and numerous other educational establishments. Every September it holds the biggest *trade fair* not merely in Greece but in the whole Balkans. It is also a large *commercial port*, the gateway to the Balkans from the Mediterranean.

Built in the vicinity of the site of ancient Therme, Thessaloníki has a long history that is generally agreed to have begun in the year 316 BC. This was when king Cassander amalgamated a number of scattered settlements in the area into a single urban centre, giving it the name of his wife Thessalonica, who was also the sister of Alexander the Great. In the centuries that followed, the city was to experience periods of great prosperity but also of adversity. Gradually it became a bastion of the Byzantine state against foreign invasion. In 1430, however, it passed into the hands of the Ottoman invader, and at the turn of the 15th century large numbers of *Span-*

ish Jews found refuge there from persecution, forming themselves into a large and prosperous community that was nicknamed 'the Mother of Israel'. Greek troops eventually liberated Thessaloníki from the Turks on 26th October 1912. Following the devastation of the *Great Fire* of 1917, Thessaloníki regrouped to become a modern, twentieth-century city. It suffered one last tribulation with the Nazi occupation (1941-1944), which was responsible for effectively wiping out the whole of the Jewish community.

This is a city with a wealth of historical monuments. Its centre of gravity, so to speak, is the Byzantine period. It has many museum collections: the major *Archaeological Museum*, the new *Museum of Byzantine Civilization*, the *Macedonia & Thrace Folklore and Ethnographic Museum*, the *Museum of the Fight for Macedonia*, the *Thessaloníki Centre for Jewish Research*, a *Museum of Modern Art*, a *War Museum*, a *Museum of Technology*, a *Cinema Museum*, and the *Municipal Art Gallery*. Also a vital part of the city's intellectual life is the *Centre for Macedonian Studies*, with its large library and its unparallelled historical and folklore archive.

Thessaloníki's historical buildings and monuments fall naturally into three main groups. The first comprises the city's fortifications and connected structures. The most celebrated of these is the *White Tower* (Lefkós Pírgos), which is the city's crest. (The tower had an earlier Turkish name, Kanlí Kule, which means 'Bloody Tower').

Thessaloniki, the church of St George. This building, also known as the Rotunda, dates from the 4th century A.D. Today it is a museum hosting various cultural events.

Thessaloniki, cathedral church of St Demetrius. Though much altered, this church of the city's saint and protector is still today a most impressive building. In it is the crypt with the saint's relics.

Built by the Venetians in the 15th century, the White Tower was a node in the city's fortifications to the S. The original walls of Thessaloníki have, incidentally, been largely dismantled; but the fortifications at their northernmost point – the complex known as the *Eptapírgio* (or 'Seven Towers') – survives virtually intact, and was being used not so very many years ago as a prison for criminal offenders and political detainees. To this first group is usually assigned that superb building the *Arch of Galerius* (the Kamára, as it is called locally), right in the heart of the modern town, a lasting reminder of Roman triumphal processions.

The second group of monuments in Thessaloníki comprises the many ecclesiastical buildings of Byzantine times. Outstanding among these is the impressive *basilica of St Demetrius*, the city's patron saint, whose relics are preserved in its crypt. This, the city's cathedral, was first built in the 4th century, but has been rebuilt time and again before taking its present form. Other major churches are the domed *basilica of Ágia Sophía* (probably 7th c.); the 4th-century *Rotunda of St George*, now in use as a museum; the 5th- or 6th-century *basilica of the Ahiropíitos* (the church 'not made with human hands'); the 11th-century cross-in-square church of *Panagía Halkéon* (Our Lady of the Coppersmiths); the typically Byzantine *St Katherine's* and *St Panteleimon* (both 12th-century) and *Agíon Apostólon* (probably 14th-century); the *Vlatádon monastery* (14th-century), with its extensive library; and *St Nicholas Orfanoú* (probably 14th-century), whose frescoes survive.

The third group comprises a whole host of miscellaneous post-Byzantine monuments, such as the *Alaca Imaret and Yeni Cami mosques* and their precincts, the *Turkish Baths* (the Hammam), or the *Hypapante* church.

The town plan of Thessaloníki as a whole also includes the outlying municipality of Kalamariá, with its pretty seafront, the *Aretsoú*. In the vicinity there are numerous substantial settlements. To the S and E, between the city and the district around mt Hortiátis and Lake Koróneia, there are three popular summer seaside resorts: *Peraía, Ágia Triáda*, and *Nea Mihaniónas*. Further inland are Epanomí, Trílofo, *Vasiliká*, Nea Redestós, Thérmi, *Panórama*, and Asvestohóri ('Limehouse'). To the west, between the rivers Gallikós and Loudías, places of note are Diavatá, *Nea Magnisía*, Síndos, Halástra, *Nea Mesimvría*, Vathílakkos, Halkídon, and Koúfalia.

The central and E part of the prefecture is more sparsely populated, and offers itself to green tourism of all kinds. You will particularly enjoy the excursions to the *Koróni-Vólvi lake system*, an important biotope, and the mountains of *Kedrílio* and *Vertískos*. You will also naturally want to visit the coast at the *mouth of the Strimónas*, with the summer resorts of Asproválta and Stavrós.

N of the line of the two great lakes there are other rewarding places to visit. Langadás, which used to be the capital of its own little province, is world-famous for its annual tradition of 'firewalking', where on May 21st the *Anastenárides* ('Groaners') tread on live coals. Then there are historic *Lahanás, Sohós*, and other villages. Among the places of interest S of the lakes and E of mt Hortiátis, are Zanglivéri, Nea Apollonía, and Nea Máditos.

Thessaloniki, city walls. A section of the walls, which are in a good state of preservation, in the Upper Town.

PREFECTURE OF HALKIDIKI

The prefecture of Halkidikí comprises districts of central Macedonia. The term covers the southernmost part of the Halkidikí peninsula, which is bounded by the Gulf of Thérmi to the W, the Gulf of Strimónas (sometimes known as Orfanoú Bay) to the E, and the open waters of the Aegean to the S. The prefecture has a characteristic shape: three long 'peninsulas within a peninsula' – the *Legs of Halkidikí* – jut out like the udders of a cow. The westernmost is called Kassándra; the one in the middle is Sithonía; and the easternmost is Áthos, 'the Holy Mountain'. While Áthos belongs in a broad sense to the prefecture, it is at the same time an autonomous self-governing monastic state. Between the Legs of Halkidikí are two deep inlets, the Bay of Kassándra and the Bay of Áthos. On the outer edge of the third, eastern leg is the Bay of Ierissós.

The prefecture is more mountainous than not (approximately 55%), and of the areas of plain, most are to the W. Its highest peak is the formidable spike of the *Áthos ridge* (2033 m). The next highest is mount Holomón (1065 m) in the N central area. There are further substantial heights: Stratonikó to the NE, an outcrop of Hortiátis to the NW, and mt Ítamos on the peninsula of Sithonía. The system of rivers and lakes is by and large impoverished. The climate is mild and Mediterranean, owing to the beneficial effect of the sea.

View of Poligiros.
Inland capital of the prefecture of Halkidiki, this market town is in the foothills of mount Holomon. Its archaeological museums contain finds from all over Halkidiki.

Communication with the prefecture is basically by road, though it can also be reached from sea by vessels of sufficiently shallow draught. The road network within the prefecture is fairly comprehensive, but the Holy Mountain is an exception, for roads there are very few and far between.

In Halkidikí there is no major urban centre at all. Its reputation is built upon its natural beauty, and for that reason it is a highly popular tourist destination. Its capital is Polígiros (pop. approx. 5000), a modern township on the lower slopes of mt Holomón. This town's *Archaeological Museum* can be warmly recommended, for it contains finds from all over the prefecture.

When you tour the W districts of Halkidikí, you will find that habitation is most thickly concentrated in the areas along the coast. Even before you reach Kassándra, there are the rapidly developing resorts of *Kalikráteia*, *Sozópoli*, and *Néa Moudaniá*. In the hinterland of this region is a must-visit site, the celebrated Cave of Petrálona. The Neanderthal remains found in the cave still provoke controversy amongst anthropologists. From a later period there is the archaeological site of *Ólynthos*. This city enjoyed great prosperity and influence in classical times, only to be laid waste by Philip II of Macedon.

To get down on to the E leg, Kassándra, you have to pass over an isthmus – a narrow neck of land that is cut by the *Nea Potídaia canal*. Hereabouts are the ruins of the classical city of *Potidaea*, another of the victims of Philip II, but rebuilt by the general Cas-

The Petralona Cave, view of the interior. Major (and controversial) discoveries made at this site by anthropologists include the Archanthropus skeleton, making the cave famous worldwide.

Armenisti. One of the numerous wonderful beaches that make Chalcidice such a popular summer tourist destination.

Nea Fokaia. A typical scene at what is one of the prettiest spots in the prefecture.

sander and named Cassandria in his honour. From here on, the road hugs the E coast of the peninsula, which is studded with major seaside tourist resorts: *Nea Fókaia*, *Áfytos* (also found as Áthytos), Haniótis, *Palioúri*, and so on. At the end of the peninsula the road turns back NW, to hug the W coast. Among the districts it passes through are Kalándra and Posídio, where there are the remains of the classical city of *Ménde*.

In the central, mountainous region of the prefecture and along the 'middle leg', Sithonía, building has proceeded at a far more leisurely pace, there are fewer clusters of houses, and your holiday will be that much quieter. Most of the building has been on Sithonía, where the road runs past the beaches, and this is only to be expected. On the E coast here, there are major resorts at Ágios Nikólaos, Vourvouroú, and Sórti. On the W coast, there is *Neos Marmarás*, and nearby, the 1960s model tourist village of *Pórto Carrás*.

The E of the prefecture has some well-known settlements, including the pretty township of Arnaía, on the slopes of mount Holomón; the favourite seaside resort of Ierissós, with its bay, not far from the ruins of the ancient city of *Acanthus*; and Ouranoúpoli, the gateway (in the most literal sense) to the monastic state of Mount Athos*. Close by, at *Nea Róda*, is the archaeological site of *Ieró*. On no account should you miss a visit to Ancient Stagira, in the NE of the prefecture, world-famous as the birthplace of the great Greek philosopher and scientist, *Aristotle*.

Olynthus, view of the archaeological site. The city-state of Olynthus and its League enjoyed great prosperity in the classical period but were ruthlessly eliminated by Philip of Macedon.

Ouranoupoli, gateway to Mount Athos.

* Mount Athos is a special case, historically and administratively, and will therefore be dealt with in the next chapter.

MOUNT ATHOS

Mount Athos – which is to all Greeks 'to Ágion Óros' ('the Holy Mountain'), and to Greek administrators 'the autonomous Athonite monastic state' – is part of Áthos, the easternmost of the three peninsulas ('legs') of Halkidikí. It has its own capital, at Karyés.

In terms of terrain, this peninsula is wholly mountainous, and is dominated by the long ridge of Áthos (or Áthonas). This ridge reaches its highest point (2033 m) close to its SE tip, forming the two headlands of Cape Ákrathos and Cape Nimphaío. Other major features of the coast are the headland of Cape Arápis (also known as Platí) at the NW tip, and the bay of Vatopédi. The absence on Athos of human interference with the natural environment means that many *endemic plant species* have been preserved: the peninsula has a fascinating variety of trees and flora.

The status of Mount Athos is governed by *Article 105* of the Greek Constitution. In the first paragraph, it is laid down that the whole of the Áthos peninsula from Megáli Vígla downwards shall by virtue of its ancient and privileged status be a *self-governing* part of the Greek state, itself under the direct spiritual jurisdiction of the Ecumenical Patriarchate. Greek national sovereignty over Mount Athos is full and absolute – 'inviolable', to use the term adopted by the makers of the constitution: it is a feature of the Holy Mountain that every person embracing the monastic life there automatically has Greek nationality immediately he is received into a monastery, whether as a novice or as a monk. In the second paragraph of Article 105 it is laid down that land on Mount Athos shall be *inalienable* – in other words, it cannot be bought and sold – and shall be the property of the peninsula's twenty monasteries. It is forbidden to increase or to decrease the number of these monasteries. They administer the affairs of the Athonite monks

Mount Athos, view of the Vatopedi monastery.

Mount Athos, view of the Esphigmenou monastery

Mount Athos, view of Karyés, the monastic administrative capital, from the air.

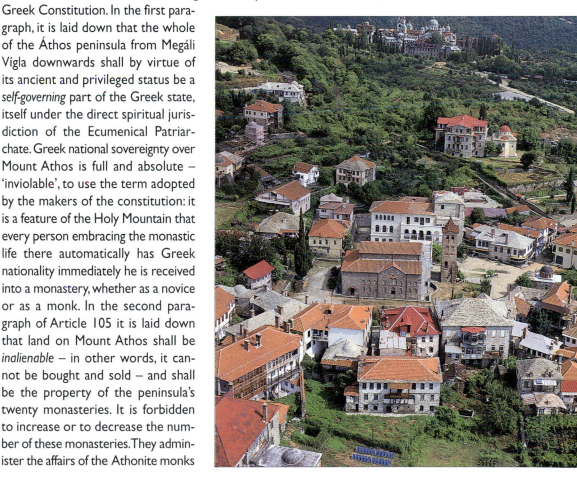

Mount Athos, general view of the Great Lavra monastery.

collectively, through their representatives, who constitute the Holy Community. No alteration whatever to this system of government is permitted, nor is it lawful for those of faiths other than Eastern Orthodox Christianity or for schismatics (Orthodox dissidents) to install themselves on Athos. Paragraph 3 provides that the definition of the *status* of Mount Athos, and its *modus operandi*, shall be as stated in its founding charter, a document drawn up by representatives of all twenty monasteries with the assistance of a representative of the Greek state. The charter has the approval both of the Ecumenical Patriarchate and of the Greek Parliament. Paragraph 4 deals with the preservation of this status by making a double distinction: the Ecumenical Patriarchate shall watch over matters *spiritual*, and the Greek state over matters that are plainly *administrative*. It is also the state's responsibility to see to the maintenance of public order and safety on Mount Athos. The powers of the state just mentioned shall be exercised (Paragraph 5 tells us) by some person appointed by the Greek government of the day as the *administrator* of Mount Athos, his rights and obligations being laid down by special legislation. Further legislation lays down what *juridical and disciplinary powers* shall be available to the monastic authorities, and what *tax and customs relief* the monastic state shall enjoy.

Life in the monasteries follows an age-old rhythm of majestic

serenity. On Athos you will find preserved all the hallowed forms of a monastic state that is attuned to the most austere Byzantine rites and traditions. Hence not only is Athos a monastic community, but it is one vast gallery of Byzantine civilization. This is reflected in many things: the architecture of the monasteries, and especially the monastery churches; the frescoes and other paintings; the woodcarvings; and other treasures of the spirit such as the manuscripts of untold value in the monasteries' archives, or the rare books in their libraries.

Only *males* are permitted to visit Mount Athos. Visitors must follow the requisite application procedure for the issue of a *passport* and so on. While they are guests on Athos, they must follow the *rules of monastic society*, rules which are in keeping with the sanctity of the place.

The twenty Athonite monasteries are mostly situated along the coasts of the peninsula. They are, in chronological order of foundation: the Great Lávra (Megísti Lávra); Vatopédi; Ivíron; Philothéou; Xeropotámou; Esphigménou; Docheiaríou; Agíou Pávlou; Karakállou; Xenophóntos; Kastamonítou (also Konstamonítou); Koutloumousíou; Agíou Panteleímonos (Russian); Hiliandaríou (Serbian); Zográphou (Bulgarian); Pantokrátoros; Símonos Pétras (also Simonópetra); Dionysíou; Grigoríou; and Stavronikíta.

Mount Athos, general view of the Iviron monastery.

PREFECTURE OF IMATHIA

The prefecture of Imathía comprises W districts of central Macedonia. It has a small outlet to the sea (on the Gulf of Thérmi) between the deltas of the r. Aliákmon and the r. Loudías. Half the prefecture (about 51%) is mountain and upland. There are two basic geomorphological units in the terrain: a broad zone of plain in the E, as an extension of the Plain of Thessaloníki, and a zone of mountains, to the S and W. The massifs in this second zone are, to the S, mt Vérmio, with its peak Chanakchi (2052 m), and to the W, the tail end of the Pierian range.

The main waterways are the r. Aliákmon, which enters the prefecture between mt Vérmio and the Pierians; and the r. Loudías, which drains the N regions. Both these empty into the Gulf of Thérmi. The climate is in general of the Continental type; but the coastal strip, with its markedly milder climate, is an exception.

Communications with the prefecture are by road, and by rail (with a branch line from the main Athens-Thessaloníki line). The road network within the prefecture is satisfactory.

The prefectural capital is Véria (found in various English spellings:

View of Naousa. This, the second largest town in the prefecture of Imathia, lies on the course of the river Arapitsa, to which is due the celebrated waterfall in the centre of the town. Not far away is St Nicholas' Grove, while Naousa is also within easy reach of the ski centres at Pigadia and Seli

Véroia, Vérroia, Berrhoea &c), with a population of approximately 43,000. Véria is 510 km from Athens and 68 km from Thessaloníki. It stands on the slopes of mt Vérmio, with the waters of the r. Tripótamos running through its streets. Visited by St Paul, the town enjoyed great prosperity in Roman and Byzantine times, as can be seen from its numerous monuments. Besides the *walls* of the ancient city, these include Byzantine and later churches: the *Palaiá Mitrópoli* (Old Cathedral) from the 11th c.; the church of *Christ's Resurrection* (1315); the 14th-c. *Agíou Vlasíou* (St Blaise's). Also eye-catching are the many old *mansions*, happily now restored, in the *Kyriótissa* quartier, and the street plan and architecture of the *old Jewish district* known as the *Barboúta*. Véria also has major museums – an *Archaeological Museum*, a *Byzantine Museum*, and a *Museum of Modern Greek Folk Art*. (Efforts are also being made to build a definitive museum in town to showcase the Vergina finds).

The archaeological site of Vergína (classical Aigai) is 13 km SE of Véria. It is one of Greece's most impressive sites. Vergína became a household name world-wide in the 1977-1978 digging season, when a brilliant discovery was made – the tombs of the Macedonian rulers. The prize find was a *royal tomb* which had largely escaped the attentions of grave-robbers and which was regarded by the excavator,

View of Veria. This is the capital of the prefecture of Emathia. It lies on the slopes of mount Vermio. Things to be seen in the town include its walls, its many Byzantine churches, commemorating the visit of St Paul, its restored mansions, and the old Jewish ghetto known as the Barbouta.

Vergina, view of the archaeological site. It was in 1978 that Vergina, a few miles south east of Veria, became a household word internationally, after archaeologist Manolis Andronikos discovered the 'Macedonian Tombs', and in particular an unplundered tomb which he claimed to be that of Philip of Macedon.

The Soumela monastery. Dedicated to the Virgin Mary, this is one of the holiest pilgrimage sites for Eastern Orthodox Christians, visited by many thousands of people annually.

Manólis Andrónikos, as that of the king of Macedon, Philip II, himself. Other major attractions in the vicinity are an Iron Age necropolis ('*the Cemetery of the Tombs*'); a *palace*; a *theatre*; the *acropolis* and its ramparts; and the *shrine of Eukleia*. Nearby is the 14th-c. *Timíou Prodrómou* monastery, also well worth a visit.

Mount Vermio, the Seli Ski Centre. This amenity has played a major part in the expansion of tourism in the region over the past few years.

The prefecture's second largest town is Náousa (pop. 20,000 approx.), 20 km NW of Véria. A smaller river, the Arápitsa, runs through the town centre, where there is a famous cascade. Náousa has much the same historical importance and charm as the capital. Its heyday was in the last thirty or forty years of Ottoman rule, when it was a major industrial centre for textiles, gold- and silver-smithing, armaments, and wine. A very short distance from the town is the sublime grove of *Agíou Nikoláou*, while a little further afield there are the two *Ski Centres* on mt Vérmio, at *Pigadiá* and *Sélio*. You will also be greatly interested in the archaeological sites in the districts to the E and S of Náousa. We can recommend a visit to Izvória, for 'the school where *Aristotle* taught' and for a *shrine of the Nymphs*; Lefkádia, for the *Macedonian tombs* named for Lyson and Callicles; and Kopanós, for the classical *theatre* and the *Macedonian tombs* named for Crisis and Anthemia.

The prefecture's third largest town is Alexándria (pop. 13,000 approx.), in the NE. It is a good base from which to explore the banks of the r. Aliákmon and the r. Loudías, and to tour the coastal zone.

Some 18 km from Véria, high on mount Vérmio, there is the village of *Kastaniá*, with its 4th-century monastery of Our Lady of the Refugees from Soumelá (*Panagía Soumelá*). The monastery is known and loved throughout the world and it is one of very few in Greece which are still prepared to offer the chance traveller a bed for the night.

PREFECTURE OF PIERIA

The prefecture of Piería comprises the S part of central Macedonia. It is washed by the Gulf of Thérmi, to the E. It is two thirds (approx. 65%) mountain. The terrain consists of two basic geomorphological units: a zone of broad coastal plain, forming the S extension of the Plain of Thessaloníki; and a zone of mountains, to the S and W. The massifs in this second zone are, on the S border with the pref. of Lárisa, mt Olympus (Ólymbos), with its peak Mytikas (2197 m), also known as 'the Pantheon'; on the W border with the pref. of Kozáni, the Pierian massif, with its peak Flámbouros (2190 m); and to the SW, in between Olympus and the Pierian range, mt Títaros (1839 m).

The coastline is relatively regular. Leaving out of account the r. Aliákmon, since it flows through no more than the N tip of the prefecture on its way to the Gulf of Thérmi, the prefecture's hydrography consists merely of a moderate number of small rivers and seasonal torrents, such as the r. Enipéas or the r. Mavronéri. On the coast the climate is mild, but it becomes harsher the further inland into the mountains you go.

Communication with the prefecture is by road (the Athens-Thessaloníki motorway) and by rail. Within the prefecture continu-

Katerini, view of the Town Centre. This thriving town, capital of the prefecture of Pieria, is relatively new, having grown up in the wake of the Greek catastrophe in Asia Minor. It has a good town plan with fine broad streets and numerous imposing buildings.

ous improvements are being made to the road network, particularly in mountain areas.

Piería's capital is Kateríni (pop. approx. 57,000), in the W central part of the prefecture, 444 km from Athens and 77 km from Thessaloníki. Kateríni is a fairly modern town. Its development came as a result of an influx of refugees in the wake of the Asia Minor Catastrophe of 1922. It is well laid out and the buildings (for instance the church of St Katherine's) are of interest. The town has a number of green areas, such as the Municipal Park or the grove of plane trees at Neokaisaría.

Travelling S from Kateríni you pass through a large number of attractive settlements (such as Nea Éfesos or Karítsa), before arriving at Díon. Here the spade of the archaeologist has brought to light an ancient Greek walled city in its entirety. The heyday of Díon was from the classical to the Early Christian period (5th c. BC to 4th c.

Díon. In this vicinity the archaeologist's spade has turned up an entire walled city, one that enjoyed prosperity from the Classical to the Early Christian period. It has a rich variety of sights, including a baths, the Villa of Dionysus, a Hellenistic and a Roman theatre, a stadium, temples of Zeus, Demeter, and Isis, Sarapis and Anubis, and a graveyard.

Platamonas. In this district by the sea are some wonderful monuments from the Byzantine period, notably this excellently-preserved castle with its majestic gateway.

AD). The site has been turned into an 'archaeological park', showcasing the ancient city in its various aspects. Dion is a wonderful place to stroll through, on pathways that meander by the riverside, in the midst of little artificial lakes and recreation areas. The things to see on site are many and impressive. They include the *Baths*; the *Hostel of Dionysus*; two *theatres*, one Hellenistic, one Roman; a *stadium*; *shrines of Greek and Egyptian gods* (Zeus, Demeter, Sarapis, Isis, Anubis); and the *cemetery*. The archaeological finds are housed in the excellent on-site *Museum*.

Continuing S, you reach the picturesque township of Litóhoro, 24 km from Kateríni. The r. Enipéas runs through the town centre. Litóhoro is a 'base camp' for climbing expeditions and hill walks on mt Olympus. The path lies through wooded landscape of spectacular beauty, which has now been designated a National Park and conservation area. Also well worth visiting is the historic monastery of *St Denys* (Agíou Dionysíou), a short way up from the town.

To the SE of Litóhoro you can reach the coast at *Leptokariá*, a pretty seaside village with a splendid beach. From there it is a short step to the seaside villages of *Nei Póroi* and Platamónas. The second of these is a summer resort with an international flavour. High above the town is a superb monument from the Middle Byzantine period, the 10th-century *castle city*. This boasts an imposing *main gate*, a medieval *chapel*, and the remains of the *dwelling-houses* of its citizens.

If we now turn to the stretch of coast N of Kateríni, there are two particular points of archaeological interest for the traveller. One is the Neolithic settlement of *Makrigialó*, 27 km N of the capital and close to the charming modern village of the same name. The other is the ruins of Hellenistic Pydna. This was a city that played the role of catalyst in the history of Macedonia, because it had the only good harbour on this coast. It was here, in 168 BC, that the decisive *battle of Pydna* took place, when the Roman troops of Aemilius Paulus put the Macedonian troops of Perseus to rout.

Another area you will enjoy exploring is the mountainous W of the prefecture, from mt Títaros to the Pierian range. Well worth visiting are villages such as Ritíni, Elatohóri, Élafos, and Riákia. If you continue via *Kolindrós* and Egínio, you will eventually arrive at the *banks of the r. Aliákmon*, one of the most important biotopes in Greece.

Mount Olympus.
A part of the Olympus massif lies within the prefecture of Pieria. The picturesque little town of Litohoro is the usual 'base camp' for mountaineering expeditions, traversing the beautiful wooded landscape of the National Park, a protected area.

PREFECTURE OF GREVENA

The prefecture of Grevená was created only recently, in 1964, by combining the existing province of Grevená (detached from the pref. of Kozáni) with Deskáti and its environs (detached from the pref. of Lárisa). This is one of the Greek prefectures with no outlet to the sea, and its territory is characteristically mountainous. The main massifs are: to the W, the northern Píndos, with its highest peak at mt Voúzios (2240 m); to the SW, mt Hásia; to the SE, the Kamvoúnia range; and to the N, mt Voúrinos.

The principal waterway is the r. *Aliákmon*. This enters the prefecture from the Siátista district in the pref. of Kozáni. Fed by the waters of a considerable number of affluents, it follows a zigzag course into the prefecture's W districts, before re-entering the pref. of Kozáni. The r. Aóös also technically runs through the prefecture, but only for a very short way in the extreme E. The local climate has no effects from the sea, and is consequently Continental, with fresh summers and notably severe winters.

The prefectural capital is the picturesque town of Grevená (pop. approx. 10,000), standing on the banks of the river Grevenítis, amid

View of Grevena. This charming town on the river Grevenitis, 1650 feet above sea level, is the capital of its prefecture.

Vasilitsa, view from the Ski Centre over a snowy landscape. With thousands of visitors every year, the Centre is one of the busiest in Greece.

The extensive natural parkland of Valia Kalda. A jewel among the landscapes of the Grevena prefecture and of Greece in general, it is made for nature lovers and 'green tourism'. These visitors are enjoying a wonderful woodland walk.

Portitsa, the stone bridge.
So far from having a negative
impact on the environment, this
bridge, like others of the same
architectural school, blends in
harmoniously with the landscape.

verdant landscape. It is 417 km from Athens and is 530 m above sea level.

Communication with the prefecture is exclusively by road. The internal road network can only be said to cover the basic essentials.

The prefecture of Grevená can best be described as one great natural parkland. Thus it is ideal for nature-lovers and for green tourism. The slopes of the *High Píndos* are thickly wooded with beech, oak and pine, and to the SW they and other massifs have been designated a National Park. There are, too, the fertile valley of the Aliákmon; and enchanting little villages, caverns, and the stone *humpback bridges* so characteristic of Epirus. Above all, the people who live in this region are by tradition friendly and hospitable, which is why more and more people are coming to visit Grevená, giving impetus to new, 'soft' tourist development that poses very little threat to the environment.

One of the most typical excursions in the prefecture is the journey up to the *Ski Centre* at Vasilítsa, 1750 metres above sea level. This passes through ravishingly beautiful countryside where you can stop off at such pretty little villages as Mouranaîi, Alatópetra, or Smíxi. Then your road climbs NW to Samarína (1450 m), subject of many a lyrical description. From here you can explore the villages in the far N of the prefecture: *Kydoniés, Amygdaliés* (Quince Trees, Almond Trees) and *Ágios Geórgios*. Once upon a time these were the lairs of *brigands and lawmen*, and later they were hideouts for the irregulars in the fight for Macedonia's freedom. From here the road winds downward to the valley of the Aliákmon, and you can cross over to the E bank and look around *Knídi* and the small Neolithic settlement there.

A further place to visit in this riverine W area of the prefecture is the historic monastery of *Osíou Nikátoros*. Founded in the 16th c., this is built like a fortress: it even has its own embrasures. S of the monastery, and 860 metres above sea level, is the historic township of Deskáti.

PREFECTURE OF KOZANI

The prefecture of Kozáni comprises central and S districts of Western Macedonia, and has no outlet to the sea. It is three quarters (approx. 77%) mountain or upland. Its main geomorphological feature is its two broad plateaux: Siátista, to the W, and Kozáni, to the E. The plain of Siátista is enclosed by the two central ranges of Askí (2111 m) and Voúrinos (1621 m), which are the continuation of each other, plus the western range of Vóïo (1802 m). The plain of Kozáni is framed by, once more, the Askí-Voúrinos mountain zone and by outcrops of mt Vérmio towards the pref. of Imathía. In the SE are outcrops of the Pierian range and the Kamvoúnia range.

The main waterway is the r. Aliákmon. This cuts through the Siátista plateau and passes into the pref. of Grevená, only to return to the pref. of Kozáni, where there is a large dam at Polífitos. It then goes on its way to the pref. of Imathía, eventually to empty into the Gulf of Thérmi. The local climate is of Mediterranean type, with deviations depending on the terrain.

Communications with the prefecture are by road and air. The internal road network is satisfactory.

View of Kozani. This prefectural capital saw its heyday during the Turkish period. It is well provided with distinctive architecture; for example, the Town Hall, the cathedral church of St Nicholas, or the Vourka mansion.

View of the historic and picturesque town of Siatista.

The prefectural capital is the town of Kozáni (pop. approx. 47,500), lying on the eastern plateau named after it. Kozáni is 506 km from Athens and 141 km from Thessaloníki. The town's heyday was during the Ottoman period. It has a good number of interesting buildings and monuments: these include the *Town Hall*, the cathedral church of *St Nicholas* (1664), and the Voúrkas and Gourtsoúlis *mansions*. It also has major museum collections: an *Archaeological Museum*; a *Museum of History and Folklore*; a *Natural History Museum*; and a *Museum of the Fight for Macedonia*. The *Public Library* has several hundred rare books and historical manuscripts.

Coming away S from Kozáni, your first stop will be to see the impressive Early Christian *basilica of Agía Paraskeví*, with its superb frescoes. You can then go onwards to the archaeological site at *Aianí*, first inhabited in the Late Bronze Age and prosperous in classical and Hellenistic times. Systematic excavation in the area began only in 1983, and to date it has uncovered major architectural complexes (the *Market Place*, a *stoa*, a *reservoir*, dwelling houses, and so on), *cist tombs*, and numerous other finds now exhibited in the on-site archaeological museum.

The route continues to the banks of the Aliákmon and the man-made *Lake of Aliákmon*, which has evolved into a major biotope.

Worthwhile is a visit to the historic town of Servía (originally a colony of Serbs) and the nearby Byzantine 'bishop's church' (11th c.) at *Kástro*. In the same district is the township of Velvendós (420 m above sea level), with the artificial *hydroelectric lake* at Polífitos, and with the two churches of *Ágios Minás* (12th c.) and *St Nicholas* (1588). There is lovely countryside surrounding the town, including the '*Ravine of the Nine Muses*' and the *waterfall* at Skepasméno.

N of Kozáni is the industrial town of Ptolemaïda. Its expansion has been rapid since the 1960s, because of its huge *thermo-electric power station* servicing the national and international grid. From Ptolemaïda you can either go to Spiliá, with its *Macedonian tombs*, or look for adventure on the slopes of mt Vérmio to the E or mt Askí to the west.

The jewel of the W districts of what was once the province of Vóïo is the town of Siátista (920 m above sea level). This picturesque and historic place has some elegant *18th-century residences*: the Manoúsis mansion (1762), the Neratzópoulos mansion (1754), and the Poulkó mansion (1752). Further on are *Neápoli* and *Chotíli*, with its quaint stone *humpback bridge*.

View of Servia. One of the larger towns in the prefecture of Kozani, it is rich in history. Well worth visiting in the neighbourhood is the 11th-century Byzantine church of Kastro.

PREFECTURE OF KASTORIA

The prefecture of Kastoriá comprises the NW corner of Macedonia, and has no outlet to the sea. Its W border also forms part of the frontier between Greece and Albania. The prefecture is nearly all (approx. 89%) mountain or upland, predominantly as part of the western Píndos system. The highest massifs are, on the border with the pref. of Yánnina and the border with Albania, the Grámmos mountains (2520 m); towards the pref. of Grevená, mt Vóïo (1802 m); and in the E, the zone including the Vérnos (or Voúrinos) range, with the peak of Vítsi (2128 m), and the Askí range (highest point 2111 m). Cutting through this zone is the *Pass of Klisoúra*, giving access from the town of Kastoriá to the town of Flórina by road.

The prefecture is drained by the upper reaches of the river Aliákmon. The hub of its system of rivers and lakes as a whole is the great Lake of Kastoriá, approximately 29 km² in area. The climate is purely Continental, and the winters are very severe.

Communication with the prefecture is by road and by air. The internal road network is generally satisfactory.

The prefecture's capital and only large urban centre is the 'fur town' of Kastoriá (pop. approx. 15,000), one of the loveliest places in all Macedonia. It stands on a plateau in the N central part of the prefecture, on the W shore of the lake to which it gives its name, 555 km from Athens, and 214 km from Thessaloníki. The modern city is on the site of classical *Keletron*, which was in Roman times to change its name to Diocletianopolis and then in Byzantine times to Justinianopolis.

The attractions of Kastoriá are its wonderful natural environment and its wealth of historical monuments and architectural gems. Its prime treasure is the *Lake of Kastoriá* (also known as Orestída). Listed as of outstanding natural beauty, this is one of the most important wetlands in the whole of the Balkan area. It is rich in *bird species* and varieties of fish. The lake has been intensively developed for tourism, and on it you can enjoy a number of sports such as rowing (Kastoriá has its own Boat Race!), sailing, windsurfing, and waterskiing. As regards its archaeology, the remains of a prehistoric lake dwelling on piles were excavated at Dispilió, 7 km to the south east of the city, and a *replica* of the dwelling, built by a team of specialist scholars, is now on view in a purpose-built museum.

The city itself is a real treasure-house of historic buildings. These include the very picturesque *vernacular mansions*, usually of three storeys, their interiors richly decorated with frescoes and carvings in wood. From the Byzantine period there are the *city walls* and a

Kastoria, the 'fur town'. Kastoria is one of the most charming places in Greece. Its trade mark is its lake, Orestida. This has been declared an area of natural beauty and is one of the major wetlands in the Balkans. Kastoria is a treasure trove of architectural masterpieces; its buildings are utterly charming and it has important Byzantine churches.

Kastoria, the Nerantzi Mansion, a splendid example of the town's architecture.

great number of churches. The most venerable of the latter are All Saints' (*Agíon Anargyron*) (1000 AD); *St Stephen's*; the *Panagía Koumbelídiki* (10th c.); the *Taxiárhis* (10th c.); *St Nicholas Kasnitzí* (12th c.); and *St Athanasius* (1385). To these should be added the nearby *Panagía Mavriótissa* monastery (1081-1118). In the city's important *Museum of Byzantine Art* there are collections of *icons* dating from the 12th to the 17th century; *mosaics*, works of *sculpture*, and *wood carvings*; not to mention ecclesiastical items and manuscripts. You should also visit the *Folk Museum*, with its display of folk dress, costumes, and tools used in the local *fur trade*.

Other places to visit in the neighbourhood of Kastoriá are *Árgos Orestikó*, said not improbably to have been the cradle of the ancient Macedonian state, and today a garrison town with a civilian airport; the pretty villages of Apóskepos and Sidirohóri; Korisós, Klisoúra, Voiatsikó, and Mesopotamía. There are a number of other attractive villages in the W of the prefecture, notably Dipotamiá, Nestóri, Grámmos, and Eptahóri.

The prefecture is ideal for climbing expeditions in the *High Grámmos* and on *Vítso*. Also recommended is the excursion to the *Petrified Forest* at Nóstimo, S of Árgos Orestikó, not far from the border with the pref. of Kozáni. Here you can see the *fossil remains* of land and marine flora, a geological reminder of how life was twenty million years ago.

PREFECTURE OF FLORINA

The prefecture of Flórina comprises the N regions of West Macedonia. Its border forms part of the Greek border with Albania, to the W, and part of the Greek border with the Former Yugoslav Republic of Makedónija (FYROM), to the N.

The prefecture is three quarters (74% approx.) mountain. Its highest massif, in the NE corner, on the borders with the pref. of Pélla and with FYROM, is Vóras, with the peak of Kaikmatsalán (2534 m). To the WSW, forming a natural boundary with the pref. of Kastoriá, are the heights of mt Vérnos, with its peak of Vítsi (2128 m); to the NW, mt Varnoús, the highest point of which on Greek soil is 2177 m above sea level. Varnoús runs out to the SW in the massif of Triklário, with its peak of Kaló Neró, 'Good Water' (2156 m): this forms a natural dam for the Préspes region.

The prefecture is blessed with a multitude of lakes both large and small. The most important of these is the Préspes system, consisting of the *Great Préspa Lake* and the *Little Préspa Lake*. Only a small part of the Great Préspa is in Greek territory; the bulk of it is in Albania and FYROM. The Little Préspa is virtually all in Greek territory, excepting a very small stretch, in the SW corner, that belongs

View of Florina. This town, the capital of its prefecture, lies on the upland edge of mounts Varnous and Vernos. Here the visitor can admire the many admirable examples of Macedonian architecture. Also worth visiting are the archaeological site on the hill of Agios Panteleimon, the Archaeological Museum, the Byzantine Museum, and the Museum of Modern Art.

View of the lakeland of Prespes. This beautiful landscape is also one of the major European biotopes, a protected area under the Ramsar Agreement. Its tranquillity is favourable to the development of green tourism here.

to Albania. Other major lakes – and they are all in the SE – are Begorítida, shared with the pref. of Pélla; Límni Petrón; Himadítida; and Zázari. The prefecture has a Continental type climate, with harsh winters and frequent rainfall: this encourages the *wealth of forests and flora* that flourish in the mountains.

Communication with the prefecture is by road and rail.

The capital and largest urban centre is Flórina (pop. approx. 15,000), 573 km from Athens and 160 km from Thessaloníki. It lies on the banks of the river Sakoulévas, in the verdant foothills where mts Varnoús and Vérnos run out. Flórina is a particularly attractive town, with remarkable examples of the vernacular building style of Macedonia. It has a busy cultural life, with a large number of annual events. The town's working museums include an *Archaeological Museum*, with pottery from prehistoric times; a *Museum of Modern Art*, opened in 1977 and containing paintings, sculpture and other media; the *Public Library*; a *zoo*; and a *Game Farm* where animals are bred for venison &c. Flórina also has its own *Ski Centre*, in the village of *Vígla*, 19 km away.

The prefecture's second largest urban centre is the township of

Amíntaio (pop. approx. 4000), 40 km SE of Flórina. The area is one of considerable archaeological interest, with sites including an Early Iron Age settlement, with graveyard; and the ruins of a Hellenistic city at modern *Pétres*. There are also pleasant excursions to be made to nearby *Lake Vegorítida*, and to the picturesque village of *Ágios Panteleímon* on its shores, and to the 'Lake of Rocks', *Límni Petrón*.

The prefecture of Flórina is a veritable paradise for nature-lovers. The *Varnoús-Triklário-Préspes* triangle is an ideal region for green tourism, and has indeed been designated a National Park. There is a great variety of tree cover on its mountain and upland slopes: oak, maple, beech, cedar, fir, and so on. It has an equally rich local fauna: there is much for the bird-watcher to enjoy, and there are also wild mammals such as wolves and bears.

The Préspes lakes offer the same, if not still greater interest. Not only is the landscape of outstanding beauty, but this is one of Europe's leading biotopes, protected under the Ramsar Agreement. Here you will find herons, cormorants, Edward Lear's silver and rose pelicans, the grey goose, and wild duck, nor is that all. The region is

Nymfeo. This pretty village is on the eastern slopes of mount Vernos. It is rapidly becoming a centre of 'green tourism' and 'conference tourism'. Nearby is the Arcturus Bear Park, a refuge for the European brown bear.

Prespes, church of St Achillius. This ruined three-aisled basilica, which once had a timber roof, was built at the turn of the 10th century. It is one of the major religious monuments in the Prespes area.

a very tranquil one, with environmentally sustainable tourist development. Good places to stay are lakeside hamlets such as Ágios Germanós, Psarádes, and Mikrolímni. This 'lake district' also has its historic ecclesiastical buildings: the *skete* (ascetic's dwelling) of *Mikrís Análipsis*, next to Great Préspa, and the church of *St Achillius* on an island in the middle of Little Préspa.

Other favoured all-the-year-round green tourism destinations are the *Vóra* massif in the NW and the mountain region of *Vérnos* in its entirety. At the E end of Vérnos, some 52 km from Flórina, is the old-world settlement of Nymfaío, a conservation area. This is rapidly becoming a centre for environmental and for conference tourism. It is in this district that you will find the *Arcturus Centre* for the protection and rehabilitation of the European brown bear.

PREFECTURE OF PELLA

The prefecture of Pélla comprises N districts of central Macedonia, and has not outlet to the sea. Its N border also forms part of the frontier between Greece and the Former Yugoslav Republic of Makedonija (FYROM).

The prefecture is approximately 60% mountain. The main massifs are, in the NW corner, Vóras with its peak of Kaïkmatsalán (2534 m); and, on the E border with the pref. of Kilkís, Páïko with its peak of Poléti (1650 m), plus the outcrops of mt Vérmio. These massifs frame the two great plains where most of the economic activity in the prefecture takes place: the plain of Yannitsá, in the SE, and the plain of Almopías (also known as Aridaía), in the central part.

There is a complex system of rivers, lakes and streams. Various major works have been carried out to intervene in this system: the lake of Yannitsá, for instance, has been drained. The main waterway is the r. Loudías. This makes its way towards the Gulf of Thérmi through a system of canals, eventually to empty into the Aegean between the r. Axiós and the r. Aliákmon. The pref. of Pélla also includes the N half of Lake Vegorítida (the S half belongs to the pref. of Flórina). The local climate is mild in the S plains, which benefit by the effects of

Edessa. The town is traversed by the river Edessaios, also known as the Voda, with its great water-falls, the most spectacular of which is the Karanos. Nearbv is an Open-Air Museum of Water.

the sea, but escalates to Continental in the mountain regions.

Communication with the prefecture is by road and by rail (where the main hub is Édessa). The internal road network is reasonably satisfactory in the plains and uplands only.

The capital and its second largest urban centre is Édessa (once known as Vodená). It lies in the SW of the prefecture, on a plateau at the back of which rise the foothills of mt Vérmio. Édessa (pop. approx. 18,000) is 560 km from Athens and 89 km from Thessaloníki. Running through the town is the r. Edessaíos (also known as Vóda), with its great *cascades*. The most spectacular of these is at the *Káranos Falls*, near which there is an open-air *Water Museum*. The town's archaeological site is of considerable interest and contains an impressive stretch of the ancient *walls*. There is an *Archaeological Museum*, where the exhibits include mosaics, sculpture, pottery, and coin collections. Also interesting are the *Old Cathedral*, a 14th-century three-aisled timber-roofed basilica; and the former *Ladies' College*. Outstanding annual events in the town are its *flower festival* in the spring (the 'Anthestíria'), its *wine festival* in the summer, and its *tsipouro* (firewater) *festival* in the winter.

If you go W from Édessa, you will reach the pretty town of Skídra, after which the road goes on to Yannitsá. Once the capital of its own province, this is in fact the prefecture's largest urban centre (pop. approx. 31,000). The town and its environs are steeped in history. It was the heartland of the Fight for Macedonia, and the scene of the *battle of Yannitsá*, in October 1912, which led to Thessaloníki being liberated. Of the many things to see here, we single out the archaeological site at *Arhontikó*, a district inhabited ever since prehistoric times; the *Clock Tower*; the *Gazi Evrenós mosque*; and the *Cathedral*. Also rewarding is a visit to the *banks of the Loudías*, where there are rowing boats for hire.

Not far from Yannitsá is the village of Pélla, with its archaeological site. Historically, Pélla was the capital of the kingdom of Macedonia. Its heyday was from the turn of the 5th century BC to 168 BC. Of its architectural remains we would specially mention the remains of *dwelling*

View of Yannitsá. This is the largest town in the Pella prefecture. Worth seeing in the neighbourhood are the archaeological site at Arhontiko, the Clock Tower, the Gazi Evrenos mosque, and the Cathedral.

houses of private citizens, where you will find *mosaics* of rare charm; the *Royal Palace*; the *Market Place*; the *shrines of Aphrodite and Darron*; the *shrine of Demeter* (the Thesmophorion); and *Macedonian tombs III and IV* (built in the Doric and Ionic order respectively).

The prefecture's third largest town (pop. approx. 6000) is Aridaía (once known as Moglená), formerly capital of the province of Almopía. About 13 km beyond Aridaía, you reach the *spa baths* of Loutrá, set in a lush landscape, the perfect place to unwind and go for long walks.

All three of the above towns are good bases for exploring the many picturesque and historic villages in the prefecture. These include *Milopótamos*, Exaplátanos ('Six Plane Trees'), and Polikárpi. If you are looking for mountain routes and 'alternative tourism', you can strike out towards mt Páïko, or mt Vóras, which has a *Ski Centre*. Or you can make for the N shores of Lake Vegorítida and enjoy their superb countryside.

Not far from Yannitsá is the archaeological site of Pella. Historically the capital of Macedonia, Pella's heyday was from the 4th to the 2nd century. Architectural monuments of note include the remains of private houses, with some fine mosaics, the Palace, the market place, shrines of Aphrodite, Darron and Thesmophorio, and Macedonian Tombs III and IV.

PREFECTURE OF KILKIS

The prefecture of Kilkís comprises W districts of central Macedonia, and has no outlet to the sea. Its northern border also forms part of the frontier between Greece and the Former Yugoslav Republic of Makedonija (FYROM).

The central and S parts of the prefecture are part of the Central Macedonian Plain, which spills over into the prefs. of Pélla, Imathía, and Thessaloníki. Its mountains and upland, which cover barely a third (35%) of its area, are practically confined to its two W and E tips – in the W, towards the pref. of Pélla, where there are the highest of the peaks, and in the E, towards the prefs. of Sérres and Thessaloníki. The main massif to the NW, on the border with Imathía, is mt Páïko (1650 m); and to the NE, the outcrops of mt Kerkíni (Béles) and the Kroúsia range (Dysoro).

The principal waterways are the r. Axiós and the r. Gallikós. These follow a southward course, accumulating the waters of numerous affluents, eventually to empty into the Gulf of Thérmi. Other main elements in the prefecture's hydrography are the great *Lake of Doiran*, partitioned between Greece and FYROM, and the much smaller lake of Pikrolímni to the S. The prefecture has a climate of the Mediter-

Lake Doiran. This beautiful expanse of water is shared between Greece and FYROM. The surroundings of the lake are an important green tourism biotope.

ranean type, with heavy rainfall and snowfall.

Communications with the prefecture are by road (with a frontier post at Evzóni), and by rail (either en route for the frontier station at Eidoméni, or in the direction Sérres and Dráma).

The capital is the town of Kilkís (pop. approx. 13,000). This town became part of Greece only after the Second Balkan War, as a result of the historic battle of Kilkís and Lahanás in June 1913. Its buildings and town plan are modern. It is 560 km from Athens and 50 km from Thessaloníki. Chief among the things to see there is the extensive 'two-storey' *Cavern* at the hill of Agíou Georgíou. This popular tourist attraction has an imposing array of *stalagmites and stalactites*. You should also visit the post-Byzantine church of *St George*, after which the hill is named, for its excellent frescoes and other paintings. The town has three museums of note: the *Archaeological Museum* (3 rooms, with exhibits from prehistoric times onwards); the *Folk Museum*; and the *War Museum* (where the exhibits mostly relate to the armed struggle of the Greeks of Macedonia during the late 19th and early 20th century).

Other settlements of note in the prefecture are the three townships of Políkastro, an important agricultural centre and communications hub 30 km from Kilkís; Axioúpoli, with a famous Fair that goes back to the turn of the 19th century, and a *Natural History Museum*; and Gouménissa, 50 km from Kilkís, which has an

View of Kilkis. The capital of its prefecture, this is a town with a modern layout. The sites of interest are mostly on the adjacent wooded hill of Agios Georgios. They include a cave on two levels, and a Byzantine church of St George with excellent frescoes. The town has a Museum of Archaeology, a Folk Museum, and a War Museum.

attractive *Museum of Macedonian Folklore*.

From Kilkís there are many excursions to be made, depending on your interests. If you are interested in historical monuments, you should certainly visit the Early Christian settlement of nearby *Kolhída*, on the east bank of the Gallikós; the archaeological sites at *Palatianó* (Torchéli, in the Kroúsia mountains) and at *Evropós*, S of Axioúpoli; the Byzantine site of *Gynaikókastro* ('Ladies' Castle'), S of Kilkís; and the Skra district in the NW of the prefecture, where there was a decisive battle between Greek and Bulgarian troops during the First World War. There are also some important monasteries worth a visit, the best known of which is perhaps *Osíou Nikodímou* (Nicodemus the Athonite), in the village of Pentálofos, not far from Gouménissa.

In terms of natural environment, the most rewarding of the many such areas in the prefecture are the grove of *Xiróvrysi*; the village of *Metalikó*; the woods at *Pedinó*, close to Kilkís; the serene banks of Lake Doiran, with a nearby recreation area at *Hília Déndra* ('One Thousand Trees'); *Pontokerasiá*, a tourist development in the Kroúsia mountains; the very beautiful hill villages on *mt Páiko*, where the hospitality of the villagers is as traditional as the style of their buildings; the lush landscape of *Dyo Potámia* ('Two Rivers') near Gouménissa; and *Pikrolímni*, the 'bitter lake', whose waters are regarded as beneficial to health. Elsewhere in the prefecture there are a great number of spas, for instance in or around Megáli Vrísi, *Tripótamos*, Lower Theodoráki, Akrítas, Pontokerasiá, Váthi, and *Skra*.

PREFECTURE OF SERRES

The prefecture of Sérres (the older form is Sérrai) comprises the E part of Macedonia. Its northern border also forms part of the frontier between, on the one hand, Greece and Bulgaria, and on the other, Greece and the Former Yugoslav Republic of Makedonija (FYROM).

The prefecture is washed by the Aegean (by the Gulf of Strimónas), to the S. It is half (52%) mountain and upland. Its principal relief feature is the central river plain of the Strimónas, which is somewhat long and narrow, with the mountains which enclose this plain. The main peaks are, on the Bulgarian border, that of the Órvilos massif (2212 m), and Kerkíni (2031 m), also known as Béles. Between these two lies the strategic defile of Roúpel. To the W, towards the pref. of Kilkís, is the Kroúsia range, also known as Dysoro; to the E, towards the pref. of Dráma, are the Vrontoús range and mt Meníki; to the S are, towards the pref. of Thessaloníki, mt Vertískos and mt Kedrílio, and towards the pref. of Kavála, mt Pangaío.

The main waterway is the r. Strimónas (also found with the spelling Strymón). This rises in Bulgaria and enters Greece through the Roúpel defile. It is fed by the Angítes, to the E, and by numerous smaller rivers and streams, eventually to empty into the Gulf of Strimónas. Another salient feature is Lake Kerkíni, in the NW. The prefecture's climate is mild in the southern lowlands, but notably harsh in the interior, and especially in the mountains.

View of Serres. The capital of its prefecture, Serres is a spacious town with quaint localities. Its many monuments are a reminder of its stirring historical past. The town has a Museum of Archaeology and a Folk Museum themed around the Sarakatsan shepherds.

View of Lake Kerkini. Here, in one of the major Greek biotopes, the visitor can enjoy landscapes of rare loveliness. It is also possible to go out on the waters of the lake in a rowing boat or canoe.

Communication with the prefecture is by road and by rail, via Thessaloníki. The internal road network is generally satisfactory.

The capital is the town of Sérres (pop. approx. 55,000). It lies at the geometrical centre of the prefecture, 592 km from Athens and 86 km from Thessaloníki. Founded in the 12th c. AD, it is set at the foot of the wooded hill of Koulás, where there are the ruins of an ancient *acropolis* and a *medieval fort* known as 'the Tower of Orestes'. Buildings to be visited in the town and its environs include two Byzantine churches (the 11th-c. *Old Cathedral* and the church of *St Nicholas*); the historic *Timíou Prodrómou* monastery (1275-1278); and the *Chichirli mosque*. There is an *Archaeological Museum* and a *Museum of Church Art*. Sérres also has the only *Museum of Sarakatsan Folklore* in the world (the Sarakatsans are a transhumant sheepfarming ethnic community).

The SE corner of the prefecture is well worth touring, for here are the *Cave of Alistráti*; the historic townships of *Nea Zíhni* and *Rodolívo*; and the village of Próti (Küpköy, as it was known in Turkish times), birthplace of *Constantine Karamanlís*, the statesman who led Greece into the European Union. In the SW, there are the township of *Nigríta*, known mainly for its mineral springs, and various other settlements of note. In the south, in the bend of the Gulf, is ancient Amphipolis. This strategic city, founded by the Athenians under their general Hagnon in the year 438-437 BC, prospered greatly when the Macedonians took over. Systematic excavation of the site began in 1956. It brought to light major monuments, of the Byzantine as well as the classical and post-classical period. Many of the finds are exhibited in the on-site *archaeological museum*.

In the N of the prefecture are two substantial townships: Sidirókastro ('Ironcastle'), with its ruined Byzantine fortress, and Iráklia. This is an area for the nature-lover to roam, whether in the plain or on the mountains. At Vrontoú (1847 m above sea level) there is the *Laïliá Ski Centre*. You should also make sure to explore the environs of Lake Kerkíni, 45 km north west of Sérres, to the south of mount Kerkíni. This can best be done on foot or by bicycle. It will be a rewarding experience, for the lake is one of Greece's most important biotopes, with a wealth of fauna and flora. There is countryside of placid beauty to be enjoyed, or you can take a boat or a canoe out on the lake itself.

Amphipolis, view of the archaeological site. It was the Athenians, in the year 438-437 B.C., who founded this strategic city on the bend of the Strymonic Gulf. It prospered under Macedonian rule. Systematic excavation has been going on since 1956.

Serres, the Bezesteni. This outstanding 16th-17th century monument from the Turkish period was probably the work of a Greek architect.

PREFECTURE OF DRAMA

If you are not well informed but simply follow the standard road route into Thrace from Thessaloníki to Kavála, you are in danger of missing out completely on the prefecture of Dráma. That would be a pity, for a tour of the prefecture will show you much that cannot be seen elsewhere, and this is one of Greece's most beautiful and historically most interesting regions.

By and large, the prefecture of Dráma, which has no outlet to the sea, is a geographical oddity because of its conflicting sets of characteristics. It is a harmonious combination of plain and mountain; of abundant waters with abundant forest fauna and flora; of intensely opposed climatic conditions, depending on place and season; and of the sense of a secure environment in which to live, with the sense of unknown, virgin territory, nature in tooth and claw. All this, and much else, mean that the prefecture is an ideal place for a

Drama, Agia Varvara. Of all the picturesque spots to visit here, the nicest is this mini wetland in the heart of town.

vacation all the year round. It is full of places to explore, and unexpected discoveries.

The capital is the town of Dráma (pop. approx. 40,000), lying in the plains of the S central part of the prefecture. It is the hub of an efficient network of communications, with road and rail links to Thessaloníki, 150 km away, to the W, and to Alexandroúpoli to the E, and with through roads to Kavála to the S and the Greek-Bulgarian border to the N.

Dráma, a town with a long and tragic history, is today a hive of cultural and economic activity. Its buildings, its architecture, and its street pattern are a mixture of the old and the new. Examples of what you can see there are the *Springs of St Barbara*, a wetland area in the heart of the town; the *Archaeological Museum*, which though not large (with three rooms only) is excellently laid out and contains a wide range of finds from the prehistoric, classical, and Byzantine periods; the *Folk Museum* and the *Museum of Church Art*; the ruined 10th-c. *town walls*; two Byzantine churches (the 10th-c. *Agía Sophía* and the 14th-c. *Taxiarhón*); and listed buildings, which include the *Railway Station* (1895).

Going W from Dráma you soon reach the tragic village of *Doxáto*, overrun and destroyed time and again by invaders from Bulgaria, and

Mount Falakro. The whole of this region is excellent for green tourism exploration. There is also a ski centre of international reputation.

The springs of the river Angitis. This river, which Herodotus mentions, runs underground, to emerge from the mouth of a cavern. Clothed in astonishing natural beauty, it is visited by thousands of people at all seasons of the year.

a second village with a history, *Prosotáni* (classical Pyrsopolis, 'Torchtown'). If you then travel northwards, you come to the r. Angítes not far from its source, and to a *cavern* which Herodotus already knew of and which attracts thousands of tourists in every month of the year. Further on is the man-made *Lake Lefkógia*, which over the past twenty or thirty years has evolved into an important wetland, with auxiliary tourist facilities; and *Lower Nevrokópi*, a particularly pretty village which is famous in Greece for having the country's lowest winter temperatures.

Other places that will repay a visit are mt *Falakró*, 'Bald Mountain', which has a *Ski Centre* of international reputation, at *Ágio Pnévma* (1720 m above sea level); the famous *Petroúsa-Pírgos ravine*; the districts of Elatiá ('Fir'), Simída ('Silver Birch'), Fraktós, and mount Meníkio, where thick forests encourage *rare ecosystems*, and are home to many different species of birds and large mammals (the brown bear can occasionally be sighted here). One last memorable experience for the traveller is the idyllic day excursion to the *Vale of the Néstos*, a landscape of astonishing beauty. This river rises in Bulgaria, then zigzags its way ESE, widening at many points into a miniature lake, to form the border with the prefs. of Kavála and Xánthi and empty into the Sea of Thrace at its delta.

PREFECTURE OF KAVALLA

The prefecture of Kaválla, which belongs administratively to the province of East Macedonia & Thrace, comprises the NE corner of Macedonia, plus the island of Thásos. It is washed by the north Aegean. A substantial feature of its indented coastline is the great Bay of Kavála.

The prefecture is three quarters (76%) mountain or upland. Its highest massif, on the W border with the pref. of Dráma, is Pangaío (1956 m). To the S of this massif, and running more or less parallel with it, is mt Symvolo. To the E rises the silhouette of the Lekáni range. The areas of plain are mainly in the C part of the prefecture, as an extension of the Great Plain of Dráma, often as a result of drainage; and in the SE, as the plain of Hrysoúpoli. The one major waterway is the r. Néstos, which forms the border with the pref. of Xánthi. It empties into the sea as the Néstos Delta, opposite the island of Thásos. The climate is variable, from Continental in the mountainous interior, to Mediterranean on the coasts and on Thásos.

Communication with the prefecture is by road, by air, or by sea (to the port of Kaválla). The internal road system is in satisfactory

View of Kavalla. This town, capital of its prefecture, stands on the shores of the Bay of Kavalla. Opposite is the island of Thasos. The town's history goes back a very long way. Built on the site of classical Neapolis, it has numerous historical monuments, which include a fortified citadel, the sea walls, and an aqueduct. The older quarters of the town are very picturesque, with their ornate mansions. The Archaeological Museum is well worth a visit.

repair. The main Thessaloníki-Alexandroúpoli railway line, though skirting the prefecture, touches its border along a section of the r. Néstos close to Xánthi.

View of the valley of the river Nestos, with its enchanting landscapes.

The prefecture's capital and largest urban centre is the city of Kaválla (pop. approx. 60,000). This fine modern city lies on the shores of the *Bay of Kaválla*, looking S towards Thásos, 169 km from Thessaloníki and 682 km from Athens. It was built on the site of the ancient 7th-c. city of Neapolis. In the 9th century the name of the city was changed to Christoupolis. In the 15th century, when the Ottoman Turks came to occupy the city, it was changed again to its present name.

The city has numerous ancient monuments: for instance the *medieval ramparts* of its 15th-c. citadel, from which there are superb panoramic views; the *sea wall*, also part of the citadel; a 16th-c. *aqueduct* built by Sultan Suleiman II the Magnificent and known locally as Kamáres ('the arches'). Of particular interest is the picturesque Old Quarter. Here are many ornate *mansions*; old *tobacco shops*, which have now mostly been turned into fashionable cafes, bars, or night clubs; the *Turkish hostel* (known as the Imaret); and the *House of Mehmet Ali*, pasha of Egypt and founder of the Fuad dynasty. The *Archaeological Museum* will repay a visit, as will the seaside villages of the vicinity (*Kalamítsa*, Tóska, *Bátis Beach*, Perigiáli, and Palió).

Philippi, view of the archaeological site. It was at Philippi, just north of Kavalla, that the first of all Christian churches in Europe was built, by St Paul in 49 or 50 A.D. The whole district contains scattered remains from the Hellenistic, Roman and Byzantine periods.

N of Kaválla is Philippi (in modern Greek, Fílippi). Here St Paul founded the very *first Christian church* in Europe, in 49 or perhaps 50 AD. Philippi's straggling archaeological site, perhaps the most important one in E Macedonia, has remains from the Hellenistic, Roman, and Byzantine periods. Notable among the monuments are the

Kavalla, the Aqueduct. Known also as 'the Arches', this is one of the town's most familiar architectural and historical monuments.

Thasos. A view of Limenas, showing its fascinating layout of monuments (walls, market place, theatre, temples, and so on), with its good Archaeological Museum. With its numerous pretty beaches and thick woods, Thasos is a popular destination for summer holidaymakers.

walls; a *theatre* (4th c. BC); the *Roman Forum* (161-180 AD); a *wrestling ground*; and 'St Paul's Prison', actually a Roman *reservoir*. Philippi also has important *churches* of the Early Christian and Early Byzantine period. The *Archaeological Museum* contains finds from a prehistoric settlement at *Dikli Taş*, and from the town of Philippi itself.

Starting from Kaválla, you have the choice of travelling W or E. If you go W, you come to Eleftheroúpoli, a pretty place with elegant vernacular buildings in the Macedonian style. You can then tour the Nea Péramos region, where there are the remains of 9th-c. Byzantine *Anaktoroupolis* and of *Pyrgos Apollonías*, founded later, by the Palaiologan emperors. There is the great natural beauty of mt Pangaío to enjoy. If you go E, on the other hand, you will make the acquaintance of *Hrisoúpoli* and – a conservation area – the delightful woods overhanging the r. Néstos at the *Parádisos barrage*. When you reach the coast, there is the Delta of the Néstos, with its wooded banks, and the seaside village of *Keramotí*, looking across the water to the green and lovely island of Thásos.

With its astonishingly beautiful shores – such as Makríammos, Hrisí Ammoudiá (Golden Sands), Órmos Prínou (Hollyoak Bay), or Potós – and its thick woods of cedar, pine, oak, and chestnut, Thásos is surely the perfect place to holiday. The island's capital and port, *Liménas* (pop. approx. 3200) is a picturesque town. It has some very interesting monuments, including the 5th-c. BC *walls*; the ancient *Market Place*; *temples of Heracles, Dionysus, Poseidon, and Artemis*; a *theatre*; and various shrines. There is a worthwhile *Archaeological Museum* with finds dating from the prehistoric to the Byzantine period.

THRACE

PREFECTURE OF XANTHI

The prefecture of Xánthi - one of the two regions of Greece where the presence of a Greek Muslim community is strongly in evidence – comprises the W part of Thrace. Its N border also forms part of the frontier between Greece and Bulgaria. It is washed by the Sea of Thrace, to the S.

The prefecture is two thirds (67%) mountain or upland. This includes the W end of the Rodópi range and the mountains of the N and N central districts. The highest massif is Koúla, with its peak at Giftókastro, 'Gipsy Castle' (1827 m), at the point where the borders of the prefs. of Xánthi and Dráma join the Greek-Bulgarian frontier. To the E, the northern zone of mountains runs out in mt Papíki. In the central part of the prefecture there are the peaks of Ahlát Chal (1400 m) and Kamérchi (1000 m). The S districts – forming part of the Plain of Thrace, which extends into the neigh-

Lake Vistonida. This major biotope close to the Bay of Porto Lago has international protection. In it is the monastic fief of Agios Nikolaos, historically important and one of the great attractions of this prefecture. (The lake is in fact shared with the neighbouring prefecture of Rodopi).

bouring prefs. of Rodópi and Kaválla – are entirely flat.

The main waterway is the r. Néstos, which forms the boundary with the prefs. of Kaválla and Xánthi, and which empties into the Sea of Thrace opposite the island of Thásos. There are two much smaller rivers: the Xánthos, on whose banks the town of Xánthi stands, and the Kompsátos in the NE of the prefecture. The coastline is by and large flat and without harbourage. The biggest indentation is the Bay of Pórto Lágos. N of this bay, on the far side of a narrow strip of land, is Lake Vistonída (which is shared with the pref. of Rodópi). The local climate is mild in the southern lowlands, and generally harsh in the northern mountains.

Communication with the prefecture is by road (principally via Kaválla) and by rail (via Dráma). Much-needed improvements have been made to the internal road network of recent years.

The prefectural capital is the town of Xánthi (pop. approx. 46,000), which lies E of mt Ahlát Chal, 731 km from Athens. Xánthi is a town with a colourful past. The heyday of its prosperity was from the last days of the Byzantine empire (the Byzantines called it Xantheía) through the long centuries of Ottoman rule. The Old Town is a fascinating place to wander through. It is built on the sides of a hollow, and has narrow little streets with vernacular buildings. You should have a look at the Byzantine *Castle*; the *Folk Museum*; and the *Natural History Museum*; and you should also pay a visit to Xánthi's three monasteries (*Taxiarhón*, *Panagía Archangeliótissa*, and *Panagía Kalamiótissa*). The town's special atmosphere also makes itself felt with the *Old Market*, which has something of the oriental souk about it, and with the Clock Tower, dating back to 1859.

If you go S from Xánthi, via Yeniséa (Turkish Yenice) with its *spa waters*, you will eventually reach the township of *Ávdira*. Nearby is the site of the classical city of Abdera, mother of three great thinkers of ancient times: *Democritus*, founder of the atomic theory, *Protagoras*, and *Hecataeus*. Excavation began here in the 1950s, and has to date brought to light a great number of finds dating from the Archaic Age to the Byzantine period. There is an on-site *archaeological museum*.

Of the other rewarding sites to visit in the prefecture, we would especially recommend three: the *fort* at Kalíva (near the village of Ionikó, in the valley of the Néstos to the N of the prefecture), built during the reign of Philip II of Macedon, in about 340 BC; a *Macedonian grave and tomb*, dating from between 200 BC and 150 BC, in the Stavroúpoli district; and, not far from the village of Thérmes in the north east of the prefecture, a rock carving with the figure of *Mithras the Bullslayer*, a work datable to the 2nd or 3rd century AD.

Of the many beautiful spots in this prefecture, none is more

beautiful than Lake Vistonída. This is a superb biotope with an international reputation, which also contains the historic monastery dependency of *Ágios Nikólaos*, and close to it the bay of *Pórto Lágos*. To see more of the prefecture's countryside you might like to follow the *banks of the river Néstos* from the village of Galáni to Stavroúpoli, where there is a major *Folk Museum*; or to explore the mountainous zone in the N, with its vast forests, its imposing landscapes, and villages with such picturesque scenery and names as Upper and Lower Karíofito ('thick with walnut trees'), Oraío ('fair'), Thérmes ('hot springs', spa waters), Kalótiho ('good luck'), Ehínos ('prickly'), Myki, and Smínthi.

Xanthi, the Square. Xanthi's heyday, as Xantheia, was towards the end of the Byzantine period and during Turkish rule. A charming stroll can be had through the Old Town, with its quaint houses and alleyways.

PREFECTURE OF RODOPI

The prefecture of Rodópi (classical Rhodope) – one of the two regions of Greece where the presence of a Greek Muslim community is strongly in evidence – comprises the central part of Thrace. Its northern border is also part of the frontier between Greece and Bulgaria. It is washed by the Sea of Thrace, to the S.

The prefecture is two thirds (62%) mountain or upland, with the E end of the Rodópi range occupying its N and E districts. Its highest mountain massifs are both on the Greek-Bulgarian frontier: in the W, mt Papíkio (1460 m), and in the E, Megálo Livádi (1267 m). To the E, as you approach the border with the pref. of Évros, the mountains are visibly far less high (for example Síilo or Eptádendros), so that this zone is much more accessible. In the central and S parts of the prefecture is the great Plain of Komotiní.

The shoreline is by and large regular, and without harbourage. The exception to this is the westernmost section of the coast, which

Komotini, the Square.
The town is the capital of
a prefecture and also the seat
of the Democritus University of
Thrace. The numerous things to
see include the remains of the
old walls, the Cathedral Hall,
the Clock Tower, the Yeni Djami
mosque, the Imaret (charity
soup-kitchen of Ottoman times),
and old mansions.

is noticeably indented, and which does have a harbour, Vistonída (Porto Lágos) at its far end. The prefecture's hydrography is characterized by the large numbers of small rivers (Filioúri being the most important of these) that drain the N and E massifs. It also includes Lake Vistonída, which this prefecture shares with the pref. of Xánthi. The local climate is Mediterranean or Continental, depending on whether a district is on the coast or in the mountainous interior.

The prefectural capital is Komotiní (pop. approx. 44,000). This town is in the lowlands of the interior, 795 km from Athens, and 281 km from Thessaloníki. A diversion was made to the course of the winter torrent Boukloutzá, on the channel of which the town used to stand, in consequence of heavy flooding in 1960. Komotiní is a town with strong local colour: its streets run higgledy-piggledy, and there is much to see. In the centre you will find what remains of the Byzantine *walls*. The old part of the town has single-storey houses and narrow alleys. The *Old Market* is a quaint place, with little shops and dealers in second-hand goods. Public buildings include the *Bishop's Palace*, in the Byzantine style; the *Clock Tower*; the church of the

Komotini, one of the numerous mosques in the town.
Very obvious in the prefecture of Rodopi is the presence of a Greek Muslim element living harmoniously side by side with the Christian population.

Maroneia, view of the archaeo-logical site. Founded in the 7th century B.C., Maroneia still has structures both from classical times (including the theatre, a temple of, it is thought, Dionysus, fortifications, complexes of build-ings, and mosaics) and from Byzantine times.

Dormition; the *New Mosque* (Yeni Djami) and its precinct; the *Poor-house* (Imaret), a brick building; and the *mansions* of wealthy burgess-es (Tsanaklí, Stalíou, and so on). The town has its own *university*, the Democritan University of Thrace. It also has sizeable museum col-lections (an *Archaeological Museum*, a *Museum of Church History*, and a *Folk Museum*). In the nearby village of Symvola there is an ornate *Macedonian tomb* dating from the 3rd c. BC.

Of particular interest to the visitor is the archaeological site of Maróneia, in the south east part of the prefecture. Maróneia, found-ed in the 7th c. BC, became a powerful and flourishing city. This we can see from the substantial remains – not only of the ancient set-tlement (a *theatre*; what may be a *temple of Dionysus*; *fortifications*; com-plexes of *dwellings*; and *mosaics*), but of Byzantine Maróneia, which was restricted to the coastal area (important *secular and ecclesiastical buildings* &c). To the north of ancient Maróneia is Strími, where the archaeologist's spade has also brought interesting items to light.

By and large the prefecture of Rodópi has much to offer the tourist, the typical feature being, as in the neighbouring prefecture of Xánthi, the obvious presence of a Greek Muslim minority. There are picturesque villages to be discovered to the W – among them, Krovyli, *Sápes* (held up as a model of racial tolerance during the recent Olympic Games), Áratos, *Arísvi*, and *Arrianá*. Similarly, if you go E, you will make the acquaintance not only of mt Papíki – an area of rare natural beauty, with reminders of Byzantine civilization – but the township of *Íasmos*, Lake Vistonída, and the nearby archaeologi-cal site of Peritheóri, the Byzantine *Anastasioúpolis*.

PREFECTURE OF EVROS

The prefecture of the river Évros (or simply 'of Évros') comprises the E tip of Thrace. Its boundary also forms, to the E, the whole of the border between Greece and Turkey, and to the N, part of the border between Greece and Bulgaria. The prefecture is washed by the Sea of Thrace, in which the island of Samothráki (classical Samothrace) belongs to Évros administratively. A little over half of the prefecture (57%) is plain, namely the N districts, the districts right in the S, and the flood plain along the banks of the r. Évros. The mountain and upland regions occupy the SW part, towards the pref. of Rodópi, and in fact the principal massif forms the E part of the Rodópi range, with its highest peak at Sílo (1065 m).

The basic waterway is naturally the great r. Évros itself. This enters Greece from Bulgaria (in Bulgarian it is called the Marítsa). It runs along the Greek-Turkish border, with the Árdas and the Erithropótamos as its affluents, and empties into the Sea of Thrace, in the process forming a wide delta. The prefecture's climate inland

Alexandoupolis, view of the shore. In the background (left) is the White Lighthouse, the town's emblem.

The Evros wetland, one of the most important in Europe. It hosts a fantastically large variety of bird species, and has of course been declared a conservation area. It can be toured from Feres by boat with a local guide.

is Continental, with exceedingly cold winters. The island of Samothráki is generally mountainous, its highest point being mt Fengári (1802 m), but has a milder climate than the rest of the prefecture.

Communication with the prefecture is by road, rail, sea, and air. Ships run from Ágios Konstantínos (in Fthiótida) to Alexandroúpoli, calling at Samothráki on the way. There are direct flights from Athens International Airport to Alexandroúpoli.

The prefectural capital is the seaside town of Alexandroúpoli (pop. approx. 49,000), 345 km from Thessaloníki and 850 km from Athens. It is a relatively young town, with a modern urban plan; there are however some old houses from the early 20th century: these are a mixture of Levantine and European architecture. Not only does Alexandroúpoli have an airport, it is Thrace's one and only seaport. In fact its *Lighthouse* (1880) is the town's crest. To the W of the town are the archaeological site at *Mákri*, with the remains of a Neolithic settlement, buildings from the Greek and Roman periods, and the so-called '*Cave of the Cyclops*'; as well as the ruins of ancient *Mesembria*, including a *temple of Demeter* and a *temple of Apollo*, *walls*, and a *graveyard*.

If you leave Alexandroúpoli in an easterly direction, you will reach the Roman foundation of Trajanopolis, with its Roman baths. This city was founded by the emperor Hadrian in the early 2nd century, and the site also has the remains of some medieval buildings. You will then arrive at the township of Féres (Phérai). Here you should visit the *Panagía Kosmosoteíra* church, arguably the most important Byzantine monument in the prefecture. It was founded by *Isaac Komninós* in the mid-12th century. Féres is also a good base from which to explore the Delta of the Évros, taking a local guide with you if you so desire and traveling by motor dinghy. This will enable you to find your way around what is one of the largest wetland environments in the whole of the Mediterranean.

Beyond Féres you come to *Péplos*, close to the long bridge of Kípi that leads from Greece to Turkey. A short detour a little further on will take you to the Forest of Dadiá. Here there is an outstanding *ecological park*, biotope, and *Raptor Centre* where you can observe regional birds of prey: an on-site ecological hostel caters for visitors. The road then continues via *Kournofoliá*, where the monastery is well worth a visit, to Soúfli, 65 km from Alexandroúpoli. This agreeable town has some fine timber-framed *silk weavers' houses* (the *koukoulóspita*), and the *Museum of Greek Silks*, which presents the history of the manufacture of this fabric, from its origins in China around 3000 BC right up to the present day.

The next stops after Soúfli are *Laginá* and then the historic town of Didimótiho (pop. approx. 9000), 95 km from Alexandroúpoli. There is much to see here: the Byzantine *walled city* on the hill of Kalé; richly-decorated *churches*; the large *mosque* and its precinct; and the *Folk Museum*, housed in an elegant mansion. Continuing along the same road more or less N, you reach Píthio, with its *Cas-*

View of Didimotiho, with the river Evros in the background. In a town which has played its part in history, the sights include the castle fortifications (from which this photograph was taken), ornate churches, and a large mosque begun by Murad I and completed by Beyazid.

Feres, the cathedral of Our Lady, Saviour of the World. This is perhaps the most important Byzantine building in the prefecture. It was founded as a monastery katholikon (principal church) in the mid 12th century, by Isaac Komninos.

tle from the Late Byzantine period; Orestiáda, a relatively modern town with a smart urban plan; Kastaniá; and finally Díkaia, where the Greek, Turkish, and Bulgarian frontiers meet at a point.

Having got as far as Díkaia, you would then do best to begin exploring the prefecture's hinterland, which is largely flat, in order to discover its gems of landscape and history. The latter include the 2nd-century AD tombs at Lesser *Doxipára*; the megalithic tomb at *Roúsa* (9th c. BC); and the tomb at *Elafohóri* (4th or 3rd c. BC).

Samothráki is reached by ferry from Alexandroúpoli. This atmospheric island was already inhabited in the Stone Age. Colonized by Thracian natives in prehistoric times, it became the headquarters of the *Cabirian mystery cult*, specific to the pre-Greek inhabitants.

Samothrace, view of the main town. Continuously inhabited since the Stone Age, this island was the coven of the Mysteries of the Cabiri. Many of the monuments can still be seen, one of theme being the Cabiri shrine; it is also a place of much natural beauty and considerable 'atmosphere'.

Samothráki has an impressive number of well-preserved historical monuments. These include a *shrine of the Great Goddesses*, on the archaeological site at *Palaiópolis*, the heyday of which was in the 3rd and 2nd centuries BC; and an Early Christian three-aisled *basilica* of the 5th or 6th century. But it is also a place of much natural beauty: at Upper Meriá there are the *Foniás Falls*, in a wonderful wooded setting; then there is picturesque Kamariótissa, the island's one port; the little *lagoon of Agíou Andréa*; the beach of *Pahiá Ámmos* ('Abundant Sand') in the south of the island; *Kípi* ('the Gardens') to the east; and the shady plane trees and *panoramic view* at Prophítis Ilías. The nature of the island is such as to make it an idyllic place for a summer holiday.

The Venetian castle at Mytilini,
built on an earlier Byzantine forti-
fication. Part of the modern town
can be seen in the background.

AEGEAN ISLANDS

PREFECTURE OF LESVOS

The prefecture of Lésvos comprises the north Aegean islands of Lésvos (Lesbos) (area 1630 km²), the third largest of all Greek islands, and Límnos (Lemnos) (area 476 km²); together with Ai-Stráti (Ágios Efstrátios) (43 km²) and a handful of minor islets.

The island of Lésvos is very close to the coast of Asia Minor. It is irregular in shape: to the south its coasts are heavily indented, notably at the deep inlet or closed bays of Kalloní and Géri. Its territory consists of mountains and hills in the hinterland, and areas of plain. The two main heights are Lepétimnos (968 m) in the north and Ólimbos (967 m) in the south. To the north west of Lésvos lies Límnos. This too is an island with a great number of indentations in its coastline, the largest of which is the strategic harbour of Moúdros Bay in the south. The lie of the land is hilly to the west and flat to the east. It is a fertile island, with eleven million olive trees. South of Límnos is the much smaller island of Ai-Stráti. The climate of the region as a whole is by and large mild and Mediterranean.

View of Molyvos (the classical Methymna). This traditional little town on the north coast of Lesvos has a large number of listed buildings and an interesting collection of archaeological exhibits.

Communication with mainland Greece is by ferry or by air, with air-ports on both Lésvos and Límnos.

Lésvos, the classical Lesbos, has a very long history and tradition of culture. It was the homeland, in classical times, of the political thinker Pittacus (one of the Seven Sages), and the musicians and poets Sappho, Alcaeus, and Arion; and in modern times, of the great naïve artist Theóphilos and the writers Eftaliótis, Myrivílis, and Elytis. It came under occupation by one foreign power after another, falling to the Ottoman Turks in 1462 and being liberated only in 1912.

The main urban centre is the town of Mytilíni (pop. approx. 28,000), in the south west. This spreads over seven hills and has a substantial port. Among the numerous things to see in the town and its environs are the Venetian Castle, built on an earlier Byzantine fort; a classical theatre; a Roman aqueduct, at Moriá; the impressive 17th-century cathedral of St Athanasius and other traditional churches; two mosques, the Yeni Camí and Validé Camí; the magnif-icent Sáltas and Hadjisávvas mansions; and the church of St Barbara, with a rood screen carved by Halepás (1870). There are also sever-al interesting collections in or near the town: the Archaeological Museum, the Byzantine Museum, the Folk Museum, a notable Muse-um of Modern Art, the Theóphilos Museum, and Public Library.

If you go inland west of Mytilíni, you ascend the foothills of mount Ólimbos and reach the very charming little town of Agiásos. This is a centre of folk art, especially studio pottery, and has impor-tant Byzantine monuments, including a 12th-century church of the Panagía and the remains of the town's fortifications. South of Agiásos is Plomári, a well-developed tourist resort on the coast, which also produces a famous brand of ouzo. The attractions here or hereabouts include picturesque mansions, Byzantine churches, hot springs, and caves.

Another of the principal towns on the island is Polihnítos, to the east of Kalloní. There is a worthwhile museum of classical coins; the Byzantine monastery of Damandríou; the Lisvóri Tower, from Genoese times, at Skála; and not far from this the pretty village of Va-siliká, the place to which the Byzantine empress Irene was banished.

North north west of Mytilíni is the traditional settlement of Thermí, with prehistoric finds (at Kanóni) and a church of the Panagía Troulotí. Further to the north is Mantamádou, with its pretty 'seaside suburb' of Skála Mantamádou: here there is a wonderful long beach, Makríalos. After this come Cleó, with a Byzantine fort; Sikaminéa, homeland of Myrivílis; and lastly, at the tip of the north coast, Mólivos (the classical Methymna). Mólivos is a most delightful traditional township, full of history and with a surprising number of things to see, including a medieval castle, an archaeological collection, listed

Sigri, in the west part of the island of Lesvos. It is best known for its remarkable Petrified Forest, and also for its fortress.

buildings, and craft workshops. You should also visit Ámfissa, a little further west, a place connected with legends about Orpheus.

There is now a choice of roads. You can go to Sígri on the west coast, which has a castle but is best known for its remarkable Petrified Forest. Or you can go to Eresós, with its 'seaside suburb', the charming little fishing village of Skála Eresoú. The main attractions here or hereabouts are the remains of classical and medieval walls; two Early Christian churches, dedicated to St Demetrius and St Andrew; and an archaeological museum that is small but has a large number of very unusual exhibits.

No visit to Lésvos would be complete without a final excursion round the shores of the enormous Bay of Kalloní and into the hinterland, rich in archaeological finds and historic monasteries. The main settlements to visit are Kalloní itself and its 'seaside suburb' of Skála Kallonís; Agía Paraskeví, with the archaeological site at Klopedí; and Mésa.

View of Mirina, the administrative seat and main town of the island of Limnos.

The island of Límnos (the classical Lemnos) was reunited with Greece in 1912 after being occupied many times by a foreign power. It was here, at Moudros Bay in 1918, that the Treaty which acknowledged the defeat of Turkey in the First World War was signed. The island's capital and main urban centre is Mírina (the classical Myrhina), on the west coast. Its main attractions are its Castle, mainly due to Venice, and its archaeological museum, with finds from all over the island. Mírina (pop. 5200) is a town of cobbled streets, stone houses, and aristocratic mansions. From here you can make an excursion to the picturesque settlement of Moúdros, and the also historic villages of Kamínia and Kontopoúli. Near Kamínia is the remarkable archaeological site of Polióhni, with the remains of a whole well-organized settlement from the dawn of history. Near Kontopoúli are the remains of classical Hephaestia and of a shrine of the Cabiri.

Your tour of Límnos might end with a boat trip across to the charming island of Ai-Stráti, with its many beaches, all clean as a whistle, an ideal place to find peace and quiet close to Nature.

PREFECTURE OF CHIOS

The prefecture of Chíos comprises the East Aegean island of Chíos and the island clusters of Psará & Antípsara and the Oinoússes.

The island of Chíos (area 841 km²) lies opposite the peninsula of Erithréa (Karaburnu) on the shores of Asia Minor. It is extremely mountainous, the peak being Pelinaío (1297 m), in the N. There are however considerable areas of plain, along the more densely populated E coast and the SSW coast. The shoreline is comparatively regular. The island has a unique product, its mastich gum. The climate is mild and Mediterranean. Communication with Chíos from the mainland and certain other parts of Greece is by ferry or by air. There are also fairly frequent boat crossings in summer to Turkey, only six sea miles across the Çesme Boğazı.

The island was in all probability the birthplace of the poet Homer. It took the losing Athenian side in the great Peloponnesian War. Later it became a Roman possession, and subsequently part of the Byzantine *thema* (military district) of the Aegean. It was then occupied by various foreign powers – Genoa stayed longest – until

View of Chios Town. Lying on the east coast of the island of Chios, the town has a capacious harbour and does a roaring tourist trade.

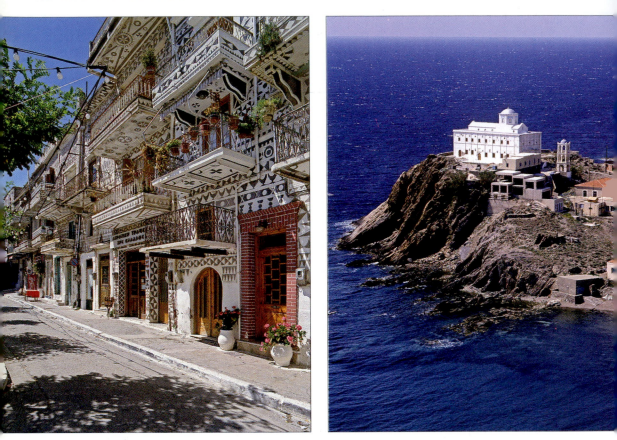

Pirgi, on Chios. This village has a startling style of black-and-white folk architecture, and a rich artistic tradition.

Psara. This little island east north east of Chios is being developed for tourism. It has just one town, also known as Psara. The main things to see are the old castle, the monastery of the Dormition of the Virgin, and traces of a prehistoric settlement.

ceded to the Ottoman Turks in 1586. Under Turkish rule it enjoyed self-government. This was no bar to its playing an active part in the War of Independence. The revenge of the Porte was swift and awful: the Massacre of Chios in 1822 which outraged international opinion. The island was reunited with Greece in 1912, as a result of the First Balkan War.

The prefectural capital is the town of Chíos (pop. approx. 24,000), on the E coast, an important port with a vigorous tourist trade. The N of the town is dominated by the Castle, built in the Byzantine period and later added to. Other notable buildings are the 5th-century basilica of St Isidore; the 19th-century church of Ágioi Víktores; the National Bank (1926); and, in the suburb known as the Kámpos, superb examples of aristocratic mansions from Genoese and more recent times. The town also has excellent museums (Archaeological, Byzantine, Folklore), an Art Gallery, and the graceful Korais Library, one of the finest collections of rare books and maps in Greece.

Out of town, you can take your pick of any of a hundred good beaches. Or you can tour the villages, often of great interest. They include the delightful Vrontádos, a seaside resort 5 km N of Chíos, with Homeric associations and the 6th-century classical site of Daskalópetra; a major biotope at Kardámila, 28 km NE; Ágio Gála, 62 km NW, with a Stone Age cave; a 13th-century church with an unusual dedication to the Virgin Mary Giving the Breast to Jesus, hence the name of its village, 'holy milk'; and a little lower down a chapel dated 1717, dedicated to St Thalelaeus, a Byzantine lawyer possibly of Lebanese origin; historic Volissós, 40 km NW, with a castle built by the great Byzantine general Belissarius; medieval Mestá, 35 km SW; Pirgí, 25 km S, named the 'painted village' because its astonishing black-and-white facades; and last but by no means least, the fine Byzantine monastery of Néa Moní, a haven of peace in the mountains.

ENE of Chíos is Psará. This island, only 42 km² in area, was to pay a fearful price for the patriotism of its inhabitants in the war for independence. In June 1824, of 20,000 islanders and refugees there, the Turks slaughtered all but 3000. Today the only settlement (pop. 420), is on the S coast. Sites to visit are the 15th-century Palaiókastro; the monastery of the Dormition; and traces of a prehistoric settlement.

The Oinoússes isles lie WNW of Chíos, close to Turkey. Their strategic position has ensured them many unwelcome visitors, including pirate fleets. The only settlement, Oinoússa (pop. 1050), was and remains a famous mother of sea captains and shipowners: it has 'captains' mansions'; richly-endowed churches; and a superb Naval Museum. There is a daily boat service between the Oinoússes and the port of Chíos.

Oinousses. This little island west north west of Chios has played a great part in Greek history, producing several leading figures. Its only town is Oinoussa, which has a splendid Naval Museum and various 'captains' houses' (mansions of notable seamen), and one or two ornate churches.

PREFECTURE OF SAMOS

The prefecture of Sámos comprises the north Aegean islands of Sámos (area 491 km²) and Ikaría (area 267 km²); the Foúrni group of islands; and a handful of other islets.

The island of Sámos is very close to the coast of Asia Minor, from which it is separated by the Strait of Samos. It is irregular in shape: to the east and north east its coasts are heavily indented, notably at the deep inlet or closed bay of Vathí, while to the S the coastline is gentler, with the open Bays of Sámos and Marathókampos. Its territory consists of mountains and hills. The main peaks are in the west: Kerketéas (1433 m) and Karvoúni, the 'Coal Lump' (1153 m). Areas of plain are few and limited. South of the main island is the small isle of Samiopoúla (now privately owned). East are the Foúrni ('Ovens') isles, with their intricate coastlines, and the other islets belonging to this group. Next in the series going westwards is Ikaría. This a long thin island – as implied by its early names 'Macris' and 'Doliche' – with a regular coastline mostly of cliffs falling sheer into the sea. The lie of the land is mountainous or semi-mountainous, the highest point being Athéras (1037 m above sea level). The climate of the region as a whole is mild and Mediterranean.

The extended town of Samos-with-Vathy. Lying in the corner of the Bay of Vathy, on the north east coast of Samos, this is the administrative seat and largest town of the island prefecture. There are numerous traditional buildings, an Archaeological Museum, an Art Gallery, a Folk Museum, and a Museum of Church Art.

Communication with mainland Greece is by ferry or by air.

Sámos is perhaps best known for having been the birthplace of Pythagoras. Its history goes back much further still into the past. The height of its prosperity was in the 6th century BC, under the brilliant leadership of the 'tyrant' Polycrates. From that time onwards the island was to be occupied by many overlords from outside: Persia, Athens, Sparta, the Ptolemies of Egypt, Rome, Byzantium, and Franks. In the 16th century it became an Ottoman possession. Only in 1834 did it attain a state of relative autonomy, though still subject to the Porte. It was reunited with Greece in 1912. The island's capital and largest town is the conurbation of Sámos and Vathí, on the Bay of Vathí on the north east coast, where there is a commodious harbour. The town has many elegant traditional buildings. You will want to see the exhibits in the Archaeological Museum, a very rich collection; the Art Gallery; the Folk Museum; and the Museum of Church Art.

From Vathí the main road runs west along the coast, passing through pleasant seaside resorts such as Kokkári, to reach Karlóvasi, a thriving coastal town with a large number of attractions (remains of a castle, historic churches, old mansions, a museum of history and folklore, and the nearby monastery of St Elijah). South of Vathí there is much beautiful country around the villages of Órmos and Marathókambos (where

View of Pythagorio. This is another of Samos' main towns. It has a noteworthy Archaeological Museum, the remains of the early classical City Wall of Polycrates, and a two-storey Revolutionary fort known as the Castle of Logothetes.

Sculptures in the Sanctuary of Hera, the main ancient shrine of Samos. It was here, by tradition, that the wife of Zeus was born. The site has important monuments including the colonnaded Ionic temple of Hera, the High Altar, the Sacred Way, and the Hekatompedos temple.

there is a Museum featuring the bones of the elephants that roamed the island in prehistoric times). East of Vathí is the picturesque fishing village of Pythagório (once known as Tigáni, 'the frying-pan'). Here you can visit the excellent archaeological museum; the remains of the walls that Polycrates built for his city, and the two-storey 'Castle of Logo-thetes'. Not to be missed, and within easy distance of Pythagório, are two wonders of classical Greece: on the hillside, the underground aqueduct built by Eupalinus to bring water into the city, one of the most astonishing technical achievements of the Archaic Age; and on the coast, the Heraion (or Shrine of Hera), the main religious focus of classical Samos and the place which was traditionally said to have been the birthplace of Hera the consort of Zeus. This archaeological site contains such important monuments of history and architecture as the Temple of Hera, a two-wing construction in the Ionic taste; the Grand Altar; the Sacred Way; and the Hundred-Foot Temple (referring to its length).

The next island, Ikaría, was originally named after the legendary Icarus, the unlucky son of Daedalus: its alternative names were Macris and Doliche. Well-watered, it was inhabited from the 7th century BC onwards. The course of its history over the centuries was much the same as that of Samos. It too was reunited with Greece in 1912.

The island's capital, main urban centre, and main port is Ágios

Kírikos (pop. approx. 1800), on the south east coast. It has a considerable archaeological collection, and among the local attractions are the remains of classical Dracanus and the nearby circular tower. Also close to the town is Thérma, a much-visited spa of international reputation whose medicinal waters are rich in radium. The two other major settlements on the island lie on the north coast: Évdilos, with a man-made harbour, good beaches, an archaeological site, and a 10th-century castle, and Armenistís, a seaside resort on the river Hálaris, which offers a gorge to explore and an archaeological site to visit on its banks.

Also worth seeing in this prefecture are the Foúrni isles, with their lush landscape of trees and flowers, their two windmills, and the village square under the plane trees. They are a good place to go fishing and enjoy a peaceful holiday.

Icaria, view of Agios Kirikos, the main town on the island. It has a good archaeological collection, and among the things to see in the vicinity are the ruins of classical Dracanus and a nearby tower. Not far away is Therma, with its radium-rich spa waters, of international repute.

PREFECTURE OF THE DODECANESE

The prefecture of the 'twelve isles', the Dodecanese (area 2714 km^2) comprises all the islands of the south east Aegean between Crete to the south west, the Cyclades to the west, the prefecture of Sámos to the north, and the shores of Asia Minor to the east and north. The twelve largest islands in this group, in order of size, are Rhodes, Kárpathos, Kos, Kálimnos, Astipálaia, Kásos, Tílos, Sími, Léros, Nísiros, Pátmos, and Hálki. The capital of the prefecture is the city of Rhodes.

The Dodecanese has always been, through the centuries, a choice target for occupation by foreign powers. By the 16th century, they were part of the Ottoman Empire. In 1912, they passed into the hands of Italy, as a consequence of the Italo-Turkish War of the previous year. Only after the end of the Second War, following a round of international settlements, did the Dodecanese become

View of the city of Rhodes. In the foreground is the Castle of the Grand Masters (the Palace of the Knights of St John).

Greek again, with official union being delayed until 1948. Today some of these islands have a vibrant tourist structure (e.g. Rhodes, Cos), while on others tourist development is still much slower. By and large the area is one of great interest for the traveller and summer holidaymaker, and is visited by many thousands of foreigners annually.

The largest and most developed of the twelve islands is **Rhodes** (area approx. 1400 km²). Roughly diamond-shaped, it lies just south of the south west coast of Asia Minor. Its capital and principal urban centre is Rhodes (pop. approx. 55,000), at the extreme end of the north coast. It is here that the tourist trade is strongest.

The city of Rhodes consists of two parts, an Old Town and a New Town. The Old Town dates from the occupancy of the Knights of St John, from the 14th to the 16th century. It has a great perimeter wall, dating from medieval times, with gateways, bastions, and embrasures. The wall runs out in the central commercial port. The chief attractions in Rhodes are the Palace of the Grand Masters (or

Rhodes, view of Lindos, on the south east coast, with the Acropolis of Lindos in the background.

View of Karpathos.
This, the second largest island
in the Dodecanese, lies between
Rhodes and Crete.

'Palace of the Knights'); the Hospital of the Knights, now housing the Arhcaeological Museum; the Art Gallery; and the 13th-century Byzantine church of the Virgin Mary of Victory, which became the cathedral church of the Knights.

The New Town is built around the Old Town. It runs out in the little harbour known as the Mandráki ('sheepfold') to the north, and the bay of Akandías to the south. In it there are many different styles of architecture and town planning. Glaringly obvious, especially near the Mandráki, is the building done by the Italians during their Occupation. Worth looking at are the Harbourmaster's Offices; the National Bank of Greece building; the Town Hall; the County Hall; the Theatre; the Market; the various Orthodox and Roman Catholic churches; and the Murad Reis mosque. West of the Old City is the archaeological site that contains the remains of Rhodes' classical legacy: a theatre, a stadium, and the temples of Delphic Apollo and Zeus Protector of the City.

If you are interested in antiquity, you should also make an excursion from the city in order to visit the island's three major archaeological sites: Ialysus, not far from Rhodes, Camirus, on the north west coast, and Lindus, on the south east coast. The nature-lover will want to tour the whole of the island's coastline, where there are uniquely beautiful beaches at, for instance, Theológou, Kalavárda,

Kastéllo, and Monólitho, in the west; and Áfantos, Kálathos, Gennádio, and Plimirió, in the east. It is also worth exploring the mountains of the hinterland, where there are many a picturesque village and the odd historical monument. We would also recommend a visit to the 'Valley of the Butterflies', not very far from Rhodes itself.

View of Kasos. This island, lying west of Karpathos, is the southernmost member of the Dodecanese.

The next largest island in the Dodecanese is **Kárpathos** (area 301 km²). Long and thin, it lies between Rhodes and Crete. The lie of the land is mountainous, with a peak at Kalí Límni (1215 m above sea level). The island has excellent beaches, ideal for summer holidaymaking: they include Ammopí, Makrís Gialós, Diafáni, and Lefkós. The main town and port is Pigádia (sometimes called Kárpathos) (pop. approx. 2000), on the north east coast. In the vicinity are the ruins of the classical acropolis of the city named Potidaea, with some grave monuments.

West of Pigádia, on the south east coast, is the lovely seaside village of Arkása, where there are the remains of an Early Christian basilica dating from between the 4th and the 6th century, with wonderful mosaics. Further north are two intensely pcituresque villages. One is Mesohóri, where there are the remains of a Byzantine church dedicated to the Holy Peace (Ágia Iríni). The other is the celebrated Ólimbos, perched in the mountains, whose inhabitants from

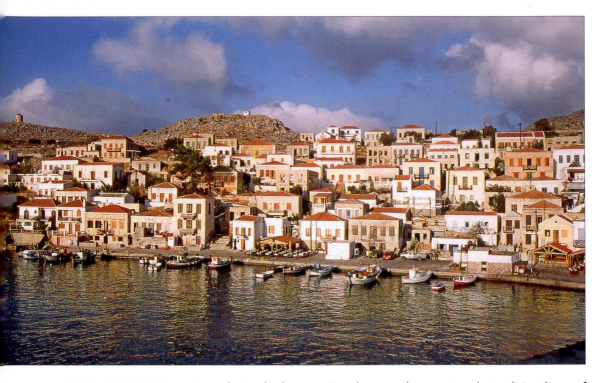

The island of Halki. Lying west of Rhodes, it was named for the copper mines that were there in classical times. The administrative seat is the charming town of Halki (also sometimes called Nimborio) built in the curve of the hill.

day to day keep up time-honoured customs and a traditional way of life. The village furthest to the north is named Trístomo, and from here you can get a boat to take you across 27 metres of water to the shepherd islet of **Sariá** (area 12 km²).

Lying west of Kárpathos is historic **Kásos** (area 66 km²). This is the southernmost island of the Dodecanese. Mentioned by Homer, it made its mark during the Greek War of Independence (1821-1829), at the start of which its fleet played a decisive role. The island was sacked to end to end and its inhabitants put to the sword by the Turkish and Egyptian military, in 1824. Its main town and port is Frí. This is a charming spot, with stone mansions and substantial archaeological and folklore collections. Other things to see on the island are the cavern at Ellinomármara (once upon a time a hide-out for the islanders during pirate raids), and the archaeological site in the district of Póli. North west of Kásos are the island of **Armathiá** (area 2.6 km²) and other islets even smaller.

West of Rhodes is the lovely island of **Hálki** (area 28 km²). It gets its name from the copper mines that were there in ancient times. Its main town, built in the curve of the hill, is Nimborió (also known as Hálki), a charming spot with its white two- and three-storey houses. The island has remains of a temple of Apollo, at Pefkiá; a Venetian castle, at Horió, the earlier capital; and a cave, at Kelliá. North east of Hálki is **Alimiá** (area 7.4 km²), an islet to

which there are boat trips, and where the excavator's spade has brought prehistoric antiquities to light.

Very close to the coast of Turkey, north of Rhodes, lies **Sími** (area 58 km²), an island with a rich history. It was the classical Metapontis (also known as Aiglé). Its main town has the same name as the island, and is in two districts: Áno (Upper) Sími and Gialó (the Foreshore). Nearby settlements are Emboriós (to the west) and Pédi (to the east). Further away, in the south, are two picturesque hamlets: Panormítis (south west) and Marathoúnta (south east). Off Sími are the two uninhabited islets of **Nímos** (5 km²) to the north and **Séskli** (2 km²) to the south. On both these, archaeological discoveries have been made. Sími itself is a very popular excursion for tourists staying on Rhodes, or on the nearby Turkish coast. The attractions are its intricate coastline and the colourful architectural ensemble of its vernacular houses. Among the things to see we would recommend the medieval castle (the 'Castle of the Knights') in the main town, and at Panormítis the legendary Taxiarchi Mihaíl monastery, where you can stay overnight, and where there is a museum of diverse objects presented by returning mariners.

South west of Sími, and an environmental paradise, is **Tílos** (area 63 km²), the Agathousa of classical times and the late medieval Piskopí. Its capital is Megálo Horió ('big village'), which, though its population is now only 240, has a medieval castle, a Museum of

View of Simi. This island lies north of Rhodes, and within a short distance of the coast of Turkey. Known as Metapontis or Aigle in classical times, it is rich in history, and is a highly popular tourist destination.

A landscape on the lush and
beautiful little island of Tilos,
west south west of Sími. It was
known in classical times as
Agathusa and in the late Middle
Ages as Piskopi.

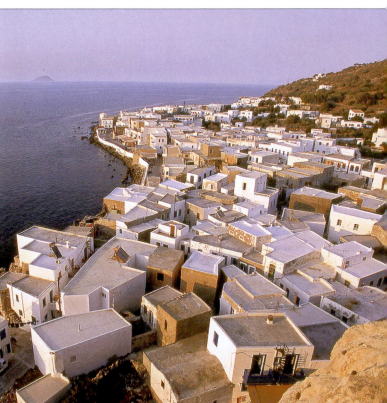

View of Mandraki, the capital
of Nisyros, in the north west of
the island. Nearby are the ruins
of the classical city, tombs, a
medieval castle, and the historic
monastery of Our Lady of the
Cavern (Panagia Spiliani).

Palaeontology, the Taxiarchi church (1827), the Harkádio Cave, and the Agíou Panteleímona monastery. Slightly larger and equally pretty is Livádia (pop. 280), with numerous little churches and white houses built in the nook of a broad bay.

If you travel in a northerly direction from Tílos, you will pass the islet of **Gaídaros** and reach volcanic **Nísiros** (area 41 km^2). In myth, Nísiros was one of the rocks that Poseidon broke off from Kos to use as ammunition in the war between the Gods and the Titans. The island's main town and port is Mandráki (pop. 680), in the north west. Towering above its blindingly white houses is the historic monastery of Panagía Spilianí, dating from the year 1600. The general picture given by the island is one of vernacular Aegean architecture, black rocks, little chapels, and sulphurous medicinal springs. There are three other settlements of any size: Emboriós, with the nearby Kyrás Monastery; Nikiá, right above the volcano; and Páli, with medicinal springs. The most striking of the rocky islets in the vicinity is **Gialí** (5 km^2) to the north, where pumice stone is quarried.

Continuing on your way north, you arrive at **Kos** (area 290 km^2). This was the homeland of Asclepius and Hippocrates, the island

Kos. This palm-lined street is one of the typical delightful spots on the island.

Kos, view of the Temple of Asclepius. The columns are Roman, in the Corinthian taste, and the temple was dedicated to Asclepius' divine father Apollo.

The town of Kalimnos (officially known as Pothia). Lying on the south coast of the island of Kalimnos, this has a fair amount of tourist traffic. Nearby are the ruins of the classical city, and a medieval castle, Chrysocheria, in which is the historic chrch of Our Lady of the Golden Hand.

where the science of medicine was born and flourished. The capital and main port, on the west coast, is also named Kos. While it still retains many elements of its historical past, such as classical Greek and Roman monuments, and Venetian and Ottoman buildings, it was largely rebuilt after the devastating earthquake of 1933. There is a great deal to see on Kos. Not only are there the classical monuments that we mentioned in the harbour district (including the classical Agora, a stoa, and shrines of Pandemic Aphrodite and Heracles); there are the Castle of the Knights, in good state of preservation; the age-old Plane Tree of Hippocrates; the Agíou Ioánni basilica; and the impressive Hasan Pasha mosque (1786) in the Platía Lótzias. Not far from the town is what is the island's major archaeological site, the world-famous Asclepium. In ancient times this was a large complex of buildings, with a religious as well as a therapeutic function, that tended to occupy a larger and larger area of ground. Note that the town has an excellent Archaeological Museum rich in exhibits.

From Kos you may like to visit the beautiful beaches to the east and north east, at Psalídi and Ágios Phokás. Or you can tour the hinterland to the west. Here there are Antimáhia (site of the island's airport); seaside summer resorts to the north (Lámbi, Tingáki, Marmári, Mastihári); the tourist spa of Kardámaina on the south

Telendos. Just off the coast of Kalimnos, and easily reachable, is this much smaller sugarloaf island, barely an acre in extent.

A landscape on the island of Leros, north of Kalimnos. Leros is lush, with many charming spots.

View of Lipsi. This small and picturesque island north of Leros is now rapidly establishing itself on the tourist map.

coast; and the particularly charming village of Kéfalo, with its Byzantine basilica of St Stephen's, the nearby remains of the classical city of Astypalaea, and the nearby Áspris Pétras cave.

North of Kos is the renowned 'Sponge-Divers' Island' of **Kálimnos** (area 111 km²), with its many pretty bays. The capital and port is Póthia (also known as Kálimnos), on the south coast. It has little white houses, handsome mansions, and a colourful array of front doors and windowframes. The main things to see are the medieval castle at Hrisoheriá, sheltering the historic little church of Our Lady of the Golden Hand); the church of the Saviour (where the rood screen is the work of the sculptor Halepás); the Kefalá Cave; the sponge-divers' workshops; a small archaeological museum; and two other museums.

From the town itself you can strike out north west to Horió, where there is a medieval castle and the church of the Panagía Charitoméni. Here it was that Kolettis raised the standard of revolt against the Turks and declared the island of Kálimnos to be Greek. Elsewhere there are the picturesque seaside villages of Pánormos, Kamári, Mirtiés, Masoúri, and Emboriós, with the gem perhaps being the verdant and highly popular settlement at Vathí.

Kálimnos is ringed by islets. Two of the larger, both of them easily accessible from the mainland, are **Télendos** (area 4.7 km²), with a population of 54, and **Psérimos** (area 15 km²) with a population of 130.

Patmos, the main town (Hora) and the Monastery of St John the Theologian, from the north west.

A little way north of Kálimnos is **Léros** (area 53 km²), a verdant island with any number of little inlets and hideaways, and with some very beautiful localities. The usual way in to Léros by sea is via its port of Lakkí. From here you can go southwards, when you will pass through the pretty seaside villages of Lepída and Xirókambos, taking in the archaeological site at Palaiókastro. Or you can go northwards, when you will come to the east coast of the island and arrive at Pentéli; Plátanos, the main town of Léros, with its medieval castle and archaeological collection; Agia Marína; and Krithóni. Other attractive seaside localities on the island are Agios Nikólaos, in the north east, and Parthéni, in the north. **Archángelos** is the most interesting of the offshore islets.

North of Léros lies a cluster of small islands of which the principal members are **Lipsoí** (area 16 km²), **Arkoí** (area 7 km²), and **Agathonísi** (area 16 km²). Tourist interest in these has been growing rapidly of late.

West of this cluster is **Pátmos** (area 34 km²), famous as the island on which St John wrote the *Book of Revelations*. The capital and main urban centre, safely away from the coast, is Hóra in the south, built in the curve of the hill. It is an imposing sight with its intricate town plan, spotless white houses in the Aegean manner, and impressive mansions. The main reason for coming to Pátmos, and one which brings thousands of visitors here every summer, is the historic monastery of St John the Theologian, otherwise known as 'the Monastery of the Apocalpyse'. Founded in the 11th century, by a monk, the Blessed Christódoulos Letrinós, this monastery contains uniquely interesting religious and historical relics. Its Library, too, has a collection of inestimable value, comprising thousands of rare books and manuscripts.

North of the town is the celebrated Cave of the Apocalypse in which, according to tradition, St John took down the divinely inspired text of the *Book of Revelations* in the late 1st century AD. It was in this same district that, in 1713, was founded the famous Theological School (Patmiáda Scholí) at which so many future leaders of the ecclesiastical hierarchy were to be students. Further north is Skála, with remains of the classical acropolis.

Pátmos is one of the eastern Aegean's little gems for the summer holidaymaker, with a number of attractive seaside villages including Melóï, Agriolívado, Váyia, Apolloú, Lámbi, Léfkes, Kastélli,

Astipalaia, the main town (Hora). The traditional cottage houses huddle all the way up to the 13th-century Venetian castle (now restored).

The island cluster of Kastellorizo. Lying opposite the coast of Asia Minor, this is the easternmost point of Greek sovereignty. The largest island in the cluster is named as such – Megisti – and is also known as Kastellorizo.

Alikés ('the saltpans'), and Psilí Ámmos ('fine sand').

Moving southwards from Pátmos you pass by a little pair of isles called **Kínaros & Levítha** and come to the outlying island of **Astipálaia** (area 97 km²). This is the westernmost inhabited island of the Dodecanese in the direction of the Cyclades. It has a weird shape: two chunks of land joined by a narrow isthmus. The beaches are superb. The island's capital, which is known alternatively as Astipálaia, Kastéllo, or Hóra ('the Borough'), is built in the curve of the hill. It is conspicuous for the little spotlessly white houses that cling to one another; a (restored) 13th-century Venetian castle; and its many delightful churches. The island's other settlements are Livádia, close to Hóra; Ágios Konstantínos, to the south; Análipsi, on the isthmus; and Vathí, to the north.

Let our tour of the Dodecanese end with the small Kastellórizo island cluster. This, the easternmost point of the Dodecanese, and therefore of Greek territory, lies opposite the south west shore of Asia Minor. The largest island in the group is **Kastellórizo** (area 9 km²): few people call it by its official title of **Megísti**. Its main town, of the same name, is a picturesque settlement with few inhabitants but a considerable number of things to see. These include a medieval fort; the remains of the classical acropolis; an archaeological museum; a folklore museum; churches; and the famous and breathtaking lovely Blue Grotto. A little way offshore are the islets of **Ro**, to the west, and **Srongíli** (more correctly, Strongilí).

PREFECTURE OF THE CYCLADES

The prefecture of the Cyclades (area 2572 km^2) comprises all the islands of the southern Aegean between Crete to the south, southern mainland Greece to the west, and the islands of the eastern Aegean to the east. The largest islands in this group are, in order of size, Náxos, Ándros, Páros, Tínos, Mílos, Kéa, Amorgós, Íos, Kíthnos, Míkonos, Síros, Thíra, Sérifos, Sífnos, Síkinos, and Anáfi. The prefectural capital is Ermoúpoli on Síros.

The islands are a treasure trove of interest for the traveller. Hundreds of thousands of tourists from abroad visit them every year, particularly in the summer months. Their attraction is multiple: their endless natural beauty, the picturesqueness of the Cycládic built environment, a good tourist infrastructure, the traditional friendly hospitality of their inhabitants, and their many historical monuments, where memories of the long-distant Greek antiquity of Cycládic and Minoan civilization and of classical and Hellenistic times coexist in perfect harmony with those of the Byzantine and Frankish middle ages, of the later years of Venetian and Turkish rule, and of the more recent period.

The most central of the islands of the Cyclades, and the one

Ermoupoli, on Síros.
The town is the administrative seat of the Cyclades prefecture. Its capacious commercial port ensured it great prosperity. 'Essential viewing' are the Town Hall (by the gifted Saxon architect Ernst Ziller), the Apollo Theatre (a scaled-down version of La Scala, Milan), the Lazareta (or Old Quarantine House), and the cathedral church of the Transfiguration.

with the largest population, is **Síros** (area 86 km²), situated between Míkonos and Kíthnos. Its principal town and port is Ermoúpoli (pop. approx. 12,000) on the west coast, built in the curve of the hill. (The earlier spelling was Hermoupolis). This town can be said to have been come to birth with the War of Independence (1821). It has a large commercial harbour, thanks to which it was to attain great economic prosperity and to flourish culturally. There were those who wanted it to become the capital of the fledgling modern Greek state. Its architecture presents a most attractive picture. Among the numerous things to see in the town are the Archaeological Museum; the superb and ornate Town Hall, by Ernest Ziller; the Apollo Theatre, built in 1864 and a replica, on a smaller scale, of La Scala at Milan; the Old Quarantine House known as the Lazaréta; the cathedral church of the Transfiguration; and the 19th-century church of St Nicholas the Wealthy.

Forming a single urban whole with Ermoúpoli is Áno Síros (the High Town), again built in the curve of the hill. This locality (pop. approx. 1100) was founded by the Venetians in the 13th century: consequently its inhabitants are still mostly Roman Catholics. Áno Síros's stage is set by its narrow alleys, white houses, stairways, panoramic views, and old-world atmosphere. The major things to see here are the Catholic cathedral of San Giorgio (1834); the Franciscan Convent; the Capuchin Monastery (1635); and the locality's main shopping street, known as the Piazza.

Not only are there these two interesting parts of the capital; numerous settlements worth a visit are to be found throughout the

Batsi, on Andros.
This is the most sophisticated
tourist spot on the island.

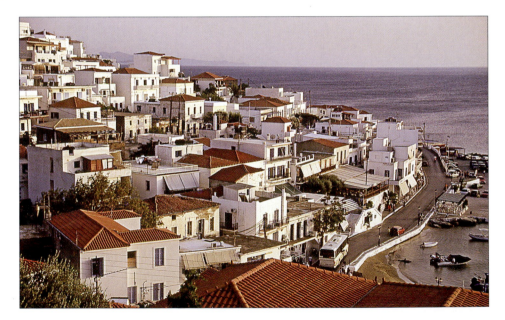

island. Síros also has lovely beaches and clear waters, which attract thousands of summer visitors every year. They include Kíni, Galissás, Fínikas, Posidonía, Mégas Gialós, Vári, and Azólimnos.

The northernmost of the Cyclades is the island of **Ándros** (area 304 km²). Its southern tip almost touches the northern tip of neighbouring Tínos. With its lush vegetation and its wonderful beaches, to say nothing of its historical monuments, Ándros is a popular place to spend a summer holiday. Its capital, also named Ándros (though more usually known as Hóra), is on the wiggly east coast, and is one great showcase of the way buildings are built and towns laid out in the Cyclades. The many attractions of the town include the evocative ruins of a Venetian castle; the fine Archaeological Museum; the superb collection in the Art Gallery; a museum of modern art which is constantly being enriched; the Embirikos Poorhouse; the church of Our Lady Palatianí; and the picturesque square known as the Platía Kaíri.

To the north of Hóra are two lovely beaches with open bays, at

Tinos, church of the Annunciation of the Virgin Mary. This building of pure white marble is the island's main town's centre of attraction. Annually, on its feast day, 15th August, tens of thousands of pilgrims converge on it. In it is the icon known as Megalohari ('Great Joy'), painted, according to tradition, by St Luke himself, and believed to work miracles. The icon is said to have been found in the second year of the War of Independence, 1822, after a vision had appeared to the nun Pelagia.

Vitáli and Makrigialí. South is the closed bay of Kórthi, with good tourist facilities at Órmos. On the west coast lie Gávrio, the island's principal port, and two major archaeological sites, Palaiópoli and Zagorá. It is well worth exploring the hinterland of the island for its wealth of natural beauty, its many charming villages, and the incomparable hospitality of the Andriotes, which goes far beyond the mere expediencies of politeness to tourists.

For the Greek Orthodox, **Tínos** (area 195 km²) is an island of pilgrimage. It is the 'home' of a celebrated icon known as the Megalohári ('Our Lady of Great Joy'). This icon is attributed to Luke, the gospel-writer, and is regarded as working miracles. It was discovered in 1822, as a result (so tradition says) of a vision which appeared to a nun named Pelagía. Today the icon is in the church of the Annunciation to the Virgin Mary, a building of pure white marble. The church is the main thing to see in the town of Tínos, on the south west coast of the island. On the feast day of the Virgin Mary, August 15th, there are always many thousands of pilgrims. Next to the church are an Art Gallery and the Museum of Artists from Tínos (including leading Greek artists such as the painters Lytras and Gyzis, and the sculptors Filippótis, Sóhos, and Halepás).

Besides the town itself, the island has many interesting places: Kámpos, with its ornate dovecotes; Exóvourgo, with a great Venetian castle; the archaeological site at Kiónia, with shrines to Poseidon and Amphitrite; Pírgos, a charming village with the house of Halepás, now a museum, workshop for sculptors in marble, and School of Fine Art.

South of Tínos lies **Míkonos** (Mykonos) (area 75 km²), one of the most popular tourist destinations of all Greek islands. Here the main attraction is the town of Míkonos (sometimes called Hóra) on the west coast. It is a model of Cycládic architecture, where the principal elements are purity of line and exclusive use of the colour white. Two especially imposing districts are Alefkántra, with its buildings jutting out over the sea, which has won it the nickname of 'the Venice of Míkonos'; and Anemómili, with its picturesque snow-white windmills. It is also very interesting to look round the Kástro area, with its church of Our Lady Paraportianí. It should be noted that other parts of the island as well as its capital, inland as well as by the sea, are undergoing tourist development.

Very close to the west coast of Míkonos are two small islands. One is **Ríneia** (area 14 km²), with a heavily indented coast and beautiful beaches. The other is **Délos** (Dílos) (only 3.4 km²), with an interest out of all proportion to its microscopic size. For this was the holy place of the classical Greek world, the place where

Mikonos, views of the main town (Chora), a model of the Cycladic style of building. Particularly striking are the sea-front quarter of Alefkandra (nicknamed 'the Venice of Mikonos), and the district of Anemomili ('Windmills').

Delos, the ancient theatre. This was the sacred island of the classical Greek world, since it was here, according to legend, that Leto gave birth to Artemis and Apollo. The island remains uninhabited, though it can be visited on a day trip.

Vourkari, on Kea. This village not far from Korresia is one of the prettiest and most popular spots on the island.

View of Kithnos. The main harbour of the island (which was known as Aphiusa or Theramnia in classical times) is Merihas, while its capital, lying inland, is Kithnos (also known as Hora), with its traditional churches in various styles.

(according to legend) Leto gave birth to Artemis and Apollo. Here, since work started in 1870, the excavator's spade has uncovered monuments of incomparable importance, which throw light on many obscure aspects of the ancient Greek world's politics, religion, social structure, and cohesion generally. You should not miss the Archaeological Museum on site, with its exhibits ranging from the most distant times to the end of the Hellenistic Age. But note: staying overnight on the island is not permitted.

North west of Síros are the islands of **Giáros** (area 17 km²) and, just off the south east coast of Attica, the now uninhabited **Makrónisos** (18 km²). Between the two lies the island that is officially called **Kéa** (130 km²), though the local pronunciation, which sounds like a sneeze, is 'Tziá'. This is a first port of call for a visitor wanting to get to know the Cyclades. The island is well developed for tourism. Its main town in the north and away from the coast, is Hóra (built on the site of the classical city of Ioulís, of which the remains of some buildings survive),. The main things to see here are a 13th-century medieval castle; the Archaeological Museum; and the many historic churches and monasteries in the area. Hóra's port, the only good one on the island, is the settlement of Livádi (on the site of the classical Koressia), on the north west coast. It is here that the famous Kouros (i.e. statue of a young man) of Kea, now in the National Archaeological Museum in Athens, was found. The island also has many interesting villages (e.g. Koúndouros, Káto Meriá, Sikamiá), areas of natural beauty and historical monuments.

Not far to the south of Kéa lies the pretty island of **Kíthnos** (area 86 km²), known in ancient times as Aphiousa or Theramnia.

Serifos, the main town (Serifos or Hora). Built in the curve of the hill, its buildings follow the style of Cycladic architecture. The capital is on the east side of the island, a couple of miles from Megalo Livadi, the island's chief harbour.

The island's claim to fame is its part in the quiet revolution of 1862 that heralded the end of king Otho's monarchy. Its main port is Mérihas, on the west coast. Its capital is the picturesque town of Kíthnos (also known as Hóra). This is inland and its chief glory is its beautiful churches, whether of austere or elaborate design. Not far from the town is the celebrated Aeolian Park with its windmills. Other places on the island worth looking at are the settlement of Driopís, with the nearby Katafíki Cave, and Loutrá, with the nearby Castle.

Continuing southwards, you reach **Sérifos** (area 73 km²). This is one of the prettiest and best developed of the Cyclades. Legend connected it with Perseus, the slayer of Medusa. Its capital, the town of Sérifos (also known as Hóra, 'the Borough'), is built in the curve of the hill, and all the houses are in the Cycládic style. The town is in the east of the island, some 5 km from its main port, Megálo Livádi. The main things to see are the remains of a Venetian castle, offering splendid panoramic views across the eastern and southern Aegean, and the post-Byzantine churches of Ágios Konstantínos, Christós (1895), and Ágios Ioánnis.

Besides Hóra itself, worth a visit are the beach and bay at Hrisí Ámmos ('golden sands') in the east, and the historic Taxiarhón Monastery in the north. Also of interest are the seaside village of Koutalás ('spoonmaker') in the south, with its nearby 'Cave of the Cyclops';

the castle at Griá; and the offshore islet (1.7 km²) of **Serifopoúla**.

South of Sérifos is verdant **Sífnos** (area 74 km²). With its beautiful beaches and emphatically Cycládic picturesqueness, this island is a favourite with summer visitors. Its capital is Apollonía (pop. 950), some 6 km from its port at Kamáres. The town has a good Folk Museum; a church of the Panagía Ouranophóra ('wearing the heavens'); and two historic monasteries nearby (Theológou and Chrysostómou). Among other places of especial interest are the Castle, with its Venetian architecture and its major prehistoric finds; the village of Artemónas, birthplace of the writer Grypáris; and Platís Gialós ('broad beach'), a celebrated fishing village, haunt of studio potters, and summer resort.

South west of Sérifos is a small cluster of islands comprising Mílos and Antímilos, Kímolos, and Políaigos, together with numerous smaller islets.

The island of **Mílos** (area 161 km²) has been inhabited ever since prehistoric times. Its name will for ever be associated with the Venus de Milo, that celebrated statue of Aphrodite which is today in the Louvre. Mílos has the geology of a volcanic island, with a heavily indented coastline, especially in the north. Its beauty, not all of which is obvious on the surface, and its Cycládic 'colouring' account for the speed with which its tourism has developed. Its capital is called Pláka (though the official name is Mílos). The attrac-

Kastro, on Sifnos. Close to Apollonia, this is one of the most intriguing settlements on the island. It is built on a rocky outcrop, with spectacular views out to sea.

Kleftiko, on Milos. The coastline of this popular island is not only pretty but of great geological interest.

Kimolos, the classical Echinusa, north east of Milos. The main town (Hora) is also called Kimolos, and its chief attraction is its medieval castle. There are many beautiful beaches.

Folegandros, view of the Chora, with its blinding white houses and the medieval castle built by Marco Sanudo at the start of the 13th century.

tions are a 13th-century Frankish castle; the Archaeological Museum and Folk Museum; and the ornate 19th-century cathedral church of the Panagía Korfiátissa. Other places to visit on the island are Adámantas, a considerable port and summer resort; Apollonía (the first A is usually dropped), with nearby Filakopí and the Papafránkas Cave; Klíma, with the nearby Catacombs and the ruins of a classical theatre; and the beautiful beach at Hivadolímni ('Lake of the Sea Urchins'). It would also be pleasant to cross over to the neighbouring islet of **Antímilos** (alternatively known as Erimómilos), an ecological conservation area sheltering the rare kri-kri also found in Crete.

The island of **Kímolos** (area 36 km²), the classical Echinousa, is to the north east of Mílos. Its name is derived from the rich deposits of chalk (*kimolía*). Its main town has the same name as the island (and is also known as Hóra). The main feature is a medieval castle. There are numerous excellent beaches. Opposite the south east shore is the uninhabited islet of **Políaigos** (area 17 km²), which is for the time being off the tourist track.

To the east of Mílos lies **Folégandros** (area 32 km²). This rocky, waterless island was already inhabited in prehistoric times, became a cult place of Artemis and Apollo, and is today moving upwards as a tourist destination. Its main town, Hóra (pop. 320), in the north, has blindingly white houses and a medieval castle built by Duke

Sikinos, landscape with castle. The island is still – for good or ill – innocent of tourist development. The gateway to Sikinos is its little harbour, Alopronia. From thence the only real vehicular road on the island leads up to the village capital (Hora).

Ios (also Nios), the classical Phoenice. It is here that Homer is said to have died. The capital and main town, also called Ios (or Hora) is in the west of the island, and has Late Medieval remains and the barest trace of the classical city.

Amorgos, the Byzantine monastery of Our Lady of Hozovo. This title refers to an icon, traditionally painted by St Luke the Gospel-writer, which came to Amorgos from Hozovo in Asia Minor.

Marco Sanudo at the start of the 13th century. The island's port is Karavostásis (pop. 60), on the east coast.

East again of Folégandros, past the islet of **Kardiótissa**, lies the island of **Síkinos** (area 41 km²). The gateway to the island is the little harbour of Aloprónia. From here the island's only road takes the traveller up to its 'borough', Hóra. This is a particularly pretty settlement, with narrow alleys, houses white all over, and stone mansions. South of Hóra is the historic Zoödohou Pigís (Fount of Life) Monastery, whose embrasures give the impression that it is a fortress.

The next island to the east after Síkinos is **Íos** (also known as Níos) (area 107 km²). This is the classical Phoenice, famous as the place where (according to tradition) Homer died. The main town, also called Íos (or Hóra), is in the west, built in the curve of the hill. It has a ruined late medieval (14th-century) castle, and some remains of the classical city (traces of walls, temple of Apollo). Other things to see in the area are the many pretty churches (e.g. Agía Aikateríni, Ágioi Anárgyri, Panagía Gremiótissa). Of the island's many good beaches, we specially recommend the bay of Agía Theodóti, in the north west, and the bay of Manganári, in the south.

Further east still is **Amorgós** (area 123 km²). Geographically, though not administratively, this island belongs to the Dodecanese rather than to the Cyclades. It is long and thin, with many good beaches, which makes it a popular tourist destination in summer. The main town, also called Amorgós (or Hóra), is on the south coast. It is conspicuous for its traditional white houses, its paved alleys, its stairways, and its windmills. The main attractions are a medieval wall with embrasures; the 16th-century Gavrás Tower, now

a museum; a number of post-Byzantine churches; and – what is Amorgós' most important historical monument – the Byzantine monastery of Our Lady of Hozovo, with its icon of the Virgin Mary thought to have been painted by Luke the Gospel-writer. The island has many other charming localities: specially worth visiting are two archaeological sites, Arkesíni in the south west and Tholária in the north east. You may also enjoy a boat trip to one of the many little offshore islets.

Between Amorgós and our next large island, Náxos, lie a host of little islands sometimes called 'the Little Cyclades', but more often 'the Koufonísia' (the 'hollow empty islands'). In the north of this cluster are **Koufonísi** itself (area 5.7 km²), now virtually uninhabited, and **Káto Koufonísi** (area 4.7 km²), presently being developed for tourism. Further south are rocky, uninhabited **Kéros** (area 15 km²), where remains of the Cycládic civilization have been found, and a number of small islets. To the west, between Náxos and Íos, are two further small islands ideally suited to the discerning follower of green tourism. One is **Schoinoúsa** (area 8 km²), with its picturesque settlements of Panagiá and Mesariá, its Frankish tower, and so on; the other is **Irakliá** (area 17.5 km²), with its picturesque settlements of Ágios Geórgios and Irakliá, its Cave of St John, and so on.

Your tour of the small islands in the area might well end with a visit to **Donoússa** (area 13.5 km²). Lying north east of the Koufonísia, this is a little paradise: an almost undiscovered summer hideaway in the south Aegean. Each of the four hamlets on the island

View of Donoussa. This island, north east of the Koufonisia, is virtually unexplored – a paradise for the summer visitor.

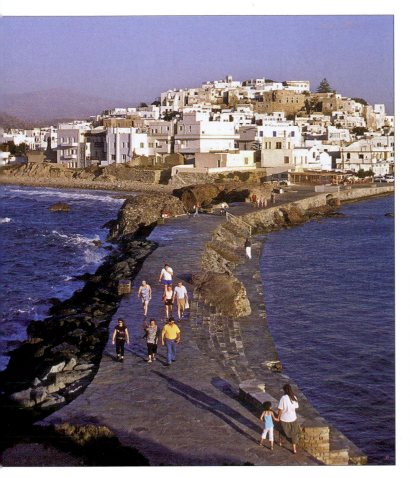

Naxos, view of the main town (Chora). Naxos blends the colours of the Aegean with up-to-date tourist facilities. 'Essential viewing' are its medieval castle, the partially-completed temple of Apollo (known locally as the Portara) on the little island of Palatia, the remnants of the classical city, Orthodox and Roman Catholic churches, and the Archaeological Museum.

(Kalotarítissa, Mersíni, Haravgí, and Donoússa, the port) has its bay and beach.

North of the Koufonísia is the massif of **Náxos**, the largest island in size (area 428 km²) of the Cyclades and one of the largest in all Greece. Inhabited since prehistoric times, it was one of the main centres of the Cycládic civilization. It was mentioned in some of the main Greek myths: it was 'Ariadne's Isle', the 'Isle of Dionysus', and the place where Zeus came to manhood. Náxos was at its height in the later Middle Ages, as the centre of the powerful Duchy of the Aegean.

The island's main town, also called Náxos (or Hóra, 'the Borough'), is on the north west coast. It has a large harbour, and also an airport. The town couples the colour of a Greek island with all the amenities which today's cosmopolitan tourist expects. Prominent among its many attractions are its medieval Castle, from which there is a fantastic view towards Paros, and well-preserved Venetian buildings; the unfinished classical temple of Apollo, standing on the

Naxos, the Portara.

*Paros, view of Naousa.
The town lies in the Bay of
Naousa, on the north of the
island. It retains many elements
of its ancient historical form,
such as the fortifications, and
is a popular tourist destination
in summer.*

*Paros, the church of Our Lady
Ekatontapyliani (or Katapoliani).
This is an important Orthodox
pilgrim centre, with thousands
of visitors annually.*

small island of Palátia; the remains of the classical city; ornate Orthodox and Roman Catholic churches; and the Archaeological Museum, with its superb collection of Cycládic art. Among the things to see in the surrounding area are, for example, the 17th-century Monastery of St John Chrysostom; the 15th-century Venetian tower house known as the Bellonia; and a Turkish fountain (the Aga Fountain).

When you tour the northern part of the island you should certainly visit the verdant and historic village of Engarés and the archaeological site of Apóllon. In the central area, there is the picturesque settlement of Apíranthos. This is a model of sensible development of historical monuments, with absolute respect for the folk tradition and the natural environment. Then too there is Filóti, where the charm of a mountain landscape blends with splendid historical monuments and churches, including the medieval Barózzi Tower, the church of the Panagía of Filóti, and the Monastery of Christ Giver of Light. The island also has wonderful beaches (e.g. Pirgáki, Psili Ámmos, Klidó, Ágios Prokópis).

A little way west of the island of Náxos is **Páros** (area 196 km²). This was another centre of the Cycládic civilization. It was the birthplace of the early classical satiric poet Archilochus. Its quarries provided classical Greek sculptors and architects with the fine purewhite Parian marble which they used for statues and temples.

The island's main town, Parikía (sometimes called Páros), is on the north west coast. It stands on the site of the classical city. It is a warren of little streets and chapels, and is crowded in summer. Among the things to see in the town and its environs are the church of Our Lady of the Hundred Doors (but the correct name is probably Panagía Katapolianí), a shrine for pilgrims from all over Greece, and its museum; the Venetain castle; the remains of the Asclepium; the historic Longobard Monastery (1638); and the very beautiful area known as Petaloúdes ('butterflies'), with its lush vegetation and plentiful running water.

Of the island's other attractions we would specially mention

Antíparos. Lying west of Paros, this island has developed its tourism very rapidly. The capital is the village of Kastro (also called Antiparos).

Náousa, on the bay of the same name in the north, with its Venetian castle, windmills, and superb beaches; the pretty seaside village of Driés, on the south east shore; and the traditional mountain village of Lefkés, with numerous churches and chapels.

To the west again, cheek by jowl with Páros, is **Antíparos** (area 35 km²). Its main settlement is called Kástro (or sometimes Antíparos), because of the Venetian fort there. The main attraction here is the cavern under the hill of Ágios Ioánnis, with impressive stalagmites and stalactites. South of Antíparos is the tiny, and virtually uninhabited islet of **Despotikó**, where interesting archaeological finds of monuments from the Early Cycladic Age have been made.

The southernmost island of the Cyclades is **Santoríni** (often known by its classical name of **Thíra**) (area 76 km²). This is a highly popular destination. Situated in the region of a by no means extinct volcano, it is the product of the massive geological disturbances that struck the southern Aegean in the remote past. Santoríni was another great centre of Cycladic civilization, and was also to be strongly influenced by Minoan civilization. But in around 1500 BC it was the epicentre of a major earthquake in the southern Aegean and suffered catastrophic consequences: a considerable part of the island sank into the sea, thus creating the great horseshoe-shaped bay on its west side. From that time on the island has been subject to a large number of destructive earthquakes of volcanic origin, the most recent being that of 1956. As a result, there have emerged the strangely-coloured islets of **Palaiá Kaméni**, **Néa Kaméni**, and **Thirasía**.

The island's capital is Firá (or Thíra, or Hóra), situated high above the west coast, with its port at Órmos Firón. The whole of the town is a conservation area. It is a most enchanting place, with its narrow little streets, its chalk-white houses, its unemphatic Cycládic churches, its Roman Catholic shrines, and of course the unforgettable view out across the bay. You might like to take the boat trip across to the Kaméni islands, where you will see a volcanic crater actively at work.

You should not miss a visit to the Akrotíri area, in the south of the island, where there is a major archaeological site with an urban complex of the Minoan civilization that was so abruptly cut short by the great earthquake of the second millennium BC, but was preserved in its entirety because buried under masses of volcanic ash. Exca-

Santorini. The island's administrative capital is its main town, Fira (also called Santorini or Hora), on the west coast; the harbour is now at Ormos Firon. The whole town is a conservation area. The visitor is sure to be enchanted by its narrow little alleys, blinding white houses, the sober Orthodox churches in Cycladic style, the Roman Catholic monuments, and the memorable view out across the waters of the bay.

vation at the site was just beginning in the 1960s and is still in progress today.

From Akrotíri you should continue to the Piríssa district on the south west coast. Here you will find the remains of the classical city-state of Thera, founded by Dorians in the 8th century BC and a flourishing place well into Roman times. This whole district is of remarkable beauty and a good area for green tourism.

In the north of the island are Imerovígli ('daytime lookout'), with its nearby historic monastery of St Nicholas; and the picturesque traditional settlements of Finikiá and Ía. From

Santorini, view of the picturesque old-style village of Ia.

Ía there are boat trips across to Thirasía.

We finish our tour of the Cyclades with a visit to the little island of **Anáfi** (area 41 km²). Its main town, easily reached from the little harbour of Ágios Nikólaos, is the pretty settlement of Hóra, whose island-style buildings and nearby Venetian castle are a magnet to visitors. There are the remains of classical Anaphe (including a temple of Apollo), and other historical monuments. A favourite place for pilgrim excursions is the monastery of the Panagía Kalamiótissa. Anáfi also has medicinal springs (at Váia) which have scarcely been exploited as yet.

Anafi. This island, which is by and large barren and waterless, is nevertheless not without interest for the traveller. The main town (Hora), with its Cycladic architecture and medieval castle, attracts a considerable number of visitors.

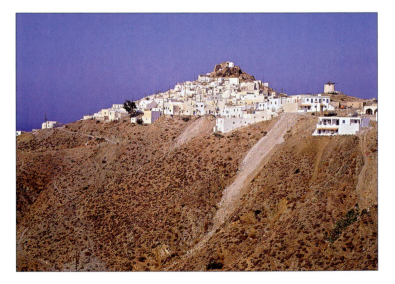

CRETE

PREFECTURE OF CHANIA

The prefecture of Chaniá comprises the west part of Crete. Its only boundary is with the prefecture of Rethymnon. It is washed by the Sea of Crete to the north, and the Libyan Sea to the west and south. Also part of this prefecture are two islands: Gávdos, the southernmost point of Greek territory, and Gavdópoulos.

The prefecture is four-fifths (approx. 80%) mountain or upland. It has substantial areas of plain, mainly in the north. Its highest massif is the range of the Lefká Óri ('white hills'), with a peak at Páhnes (2454 m): the range continues into the prefecture of Rethymnon. The hydrographic system consists of minor rivers. The coasts are heavily indented only in the north, with three great pensinsulas (Gramvoúsa, Rodopós, and Akrotíri) and four great bays (reading from west to east: the Bay of Kíssamos, the Bay of Chaniá, Suda Bay, and the Bay of Almirós). The climate is temperate and Mediterranean, but with lower temperatures and heavier rainfall in the mountainous interior.

Chania. This city has retained its earlier appearance perhaps better than any other in Greece.

Communication with the prefecture from mainland Greece is by ferry or by air; and from the other three prefectures of Crete, by road. The internal road network is reasonably satisfactory. There is also a service of coastal steamers and smaller vessels.

The prefecture's capital and largest urban centre is Chaniá (pop. approx. 55,000), on the north coast, in the east of the Bay of Chaniá. The older form of the name is Canea, and the spelling Hania is also found. This was the original capital of the Cretan State. Chaniá consists of two parts, the delightful Old Town and the newer suburbs, where modern ideas of town planning, house design, and local colour are blended in. You will naturally be interested most in the Old Town, with its picturesque quartiers (Top Haná, the Jewish Ghetto, Sintriváni, Splánzia, Kastéli, and so on); its old Venetian harbour, its narrow alleys, and its Venetian mansions, which mirror the society and history of Chaniá in a past era. These buildings include splendid examples of the Venetian, Ottoman, Neoclassical, and vernacular styles. We would especially recommend the Firkás (the Venetian fort in the harbour); the restored Venetian lighthouse; the church of San Francisco, now housing the Archaeological Museum; the Hasan Pasha mosque; the urban layout of Kastéli and the archaeological site there; the church of San Niccolò in the Splánzia quartier; and the Governor's Palace.

Starting from Chaniá, you can tour the delightful peninsula known as Akrotíri, where there are the Grave of the Venizélos Family and the historic 17th-century monastery of Ágia Triáda., founded by the Venetian family Zangaróli. Or make for the village of Suda and its bay, one of the biggest and safest harbourages in the Mediterranean. From there it is not far to Áptera, with its archaeological site, historic Vámos, where repeated risings against the Turks took place, and the lovely nearby beaches on the Bay of Almirós.

If you go west from Chaniá, you pass through several pleasant seaside resort villages (such as Kalamáki, Galatás, and Plataniás). You will want to stop at Malemé, scene of bitter and bloody fighting during the Battle of Crete in 1941 between Greek and British defenders and German paratroopers. Nearby are antiquities including a Late Minoan 'beehive' tomb. Further west are Kolymbári, with the Hodigítria Monastery (also known as Kíra-Goniás) and the Orthodox Academy of Crete; the Rodopós peninsula; and the Bay of Kíssamos. Here you should stop at the township of Kastéli – the classical Kissamus – with its many antiquities and its Venetian fortifications. Continuing west, you come to the western shores of the 'great island' of Crete, and Falasárna, a hamlet with an archaeological site and superb beaches. If you then go southwards, there are many fine seaside spots of incomparable beauty, and charming little

(opposite page)
Southern Crete, view of the Samaria Gorge, the biggest canyon in Europe.

Western Crete, the wonderful beach at Falasarna.

resort villages, especially in the harbourages of Kókkina Gremná, Stómio, and Vrouliá. At the very tip the west coast is a small, beautiful island called Elafonísi.

The whole of the south coast is similarly interesting. If you drive from west to east along it, the places you come to are Palaiohóra, well developed for tourism, with a Museum of Local History; the classical city-state of Lissus; and the Bay of Ágia Roúmeli, with the delightful fishing village of the same name, built on the site of classical Taras. Here you should most certainly make a stop, not just to go round the archaeological monuments in this area, but to see at least the start of the celebrated Samariá Gorge. This 18 km long canyon is one of the major green tourism attractions not only in Crete, but in Greece, and indeed on the planet.

Continuing east, you come to Sfakiá (the full name is Hóra Sfakíon). This is the heartland of an area which played a key role in modern Greek history, its inhabitants being intolerant of oppression by conqueror of any sort, and uprisings being frequent. On no account should you miss the excursion to nearby Frangokástello, a fort built in 1371-1374, and one of the finest examples of Frankish military architecture in Greece.

The hinterland of the prefecture is just as exciting to explore, with its wonderfully beautiful landscapes, especially on the 'White Hills' and on the Omalós plateau and its host of historic villages, invariably picturesque. These include Mourniés, a southern suburb of Chaniá and the birthplace of the Greek statesman Elefthérios Venizélos; Therissós, south of Chaniá, where the 1905 Uprising started; Fourniés, to the south west, with its spectacular cavern known as Hoiróspilos ('Boar Cave'); nearby Perivóla; Omalós, at the northern end of the Samariá Gorge; Voukoliés, south of Malemé; and Kándanos, to the south west, another village which was razed by the Nazis and the male inhabitants executed, but which has since been rebuilt.

Also part of the prefecture, as we said earlier, is the island of Gávdos, with an area of 30 km². This is the 'isle of Calypso', from Homer's *Odyssey*. It is the southernmost point of Greece, and is a perfect place for 'green tourism', being a conservation area.

PREFECTURE OF RETHYMNON

The prefecture of Réthymnon comprises the west central parts of Crete, those that lie between the prefectures of Chaniá and Iráklio. It is washed by the Sea of Crete to the north, and the Libyan Sea to the south (at the bay of Mesará and elsewhere).

The prefecture is nearly entirely (88%) mountain or upland. The only real exceptions are the areas of plain in the north. Its highest massif, which is also the highest point in the whole of Crete, is mount Psilorítis in the east – Mount Ida, as it was known in classical times – with its peak of Tímios Stavrós (2456 m). Other major mountain ranges are Kédros in the south and the end of the Lefká Óri, the 'white hills', in the west. The prefecture has many minor rivers, notably Milopótamos (also called Geropótamos), which empties into the Sea of Crete. Though climate is mild and Mediterranean, there are very wide differences between the coast and the high mountain areas.

Communication with the prefecture from Athens is by ferry boat, from the Piraeus to the harbour at Réthymnon, and from the other prefectures of Crete by road. The internal road network has fairly good coverage and is under continuous improvement.

Rethymnon, view of the wall surrounding the city and the Venetian stronghold (Fortezza) at the tip of the peninsula.

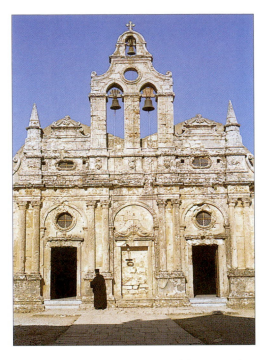

Arkadi. This historic monastery is best known for the part it played in the Cretan Uprising of 1866 (against Turkish rule). Its defenders, led by the abbot Gabriel, chose to blow up their powder magazine, at the cost of their lives, rather than surrender.

The prefecture's capital and largest urban centre is Réthymnon (pop. approx. 30,000), on the north coast. The height of the town's prosperity was under Venetian rule. In the Ottoman period it was the target of repeated harassment, which is why it was also the hub of numerous uprisings. On the west side of the town, on the hill of Palaiókastro, stands the great Venetian stronghold known as the Fortezza (built by Pallavicini in 1573). It has a polygonal ground plan, with three gates and four bastions. It contains such architecturally important groups of buildings and monuments as the Councillors' Quarters; a church of San Niccolò, which was later converted by the Ottomans into the Sultan Ibrahim mosque; and the Powder Magazines. Of Réthymnon's many other attractions, we would single out the Loggia, a great Venetian building of the 16th century, today housing the archaeological museum; the Rimóndi Fountain, with its elegant decorative sculptures; the churches of San Francisco and Our Lady of the Angels, built in the Venetian period; what remains of Musulman mosques; the *hammam* (Turkish Baths); and two neo-classical buildings, the Metropolitan church and the County Hall. Close to the town are, at Arménoi, a Late Minoan burial ground; the cave of Geráni; and the traditional village of Ádele, surrounded by olive and orange groves.

In the west of the prefecture the most notable places of habitation are Episkopí (more or less on the border with the prefecture of Chaniá); Amári, centre of a district rich in antiquities and church-

es of more recent times; Spíli, a well-known holiday resort; and the historic Préveli Monastery.

There is perhaps more to see in the east of the prefecture, where the picturesque village of Pérama is a convenient place to start from. North west of Pérama is the Cave of Melidonius, familiarly known as the Gerontóspilios ('Old Man's Cavern'). This was a place where the deities Talos, and later Hermes, were worshipped. South west are the archaeological site of Eleutherna and the historic Arkádi Monastery. Arkádi is celebrated in Greek history because in the Cretan Revolt of 1866 the monks, soldiers and townspeople defending it blew themselves up rather than surrender. There is a museum onsite.

From Arkádi you should then move on to explore Psilorítis and its environs. It was on this mountain, according to tradition, that Zeus was born, in the Idaean Cave. The largest town in these parts is Anógia, where in 1944 the Nazis destroyed the village and executed its inhabitants. Not far from Anógia is another historic village, Zonianá, where there is the Potamianós Museum of Waxworks. Also of interest is the archaeological site at Apodoúlou, with its finds from prehistoric times.

The prefecture of Réthymnon, particularly the mount Psilorítis region, is an ideal destination for nature lovers and for all who are looking for a not too noisy seaside resort. This is especially true of the south coast, on the Libyan Sea.

Anogia. This historic little town in the hills is one of the main cultural spots in the prefecture of Rethymnon.

PREFECTURE OF HERAKLION

The Prefecture of Heraklion comprises the east central part of Crete, between the prefectures of Rethímni and Lasíthi. It is washed by the Sea of Crete to the north and the Libyan Sea to the south.

The prefecture is two thirds (approx. 63%) mountain or upland. It has large areas of plain, mostly in the north (e.g. the coastal zone, the hinterland of the town of Iráklio) and the south west (the Plain of Mesará). Its highest massifs are the Asteroúsia range to the south (1230 m above sea level), and the ends of mount Psilorítis (Ida) to the west and mount Díkti to the east. The hydrographic system includes quite a number of minor rivers and winter torrents. The shoreline is fairly even, without major indentations. The climate is by and large mild and Mediterranean, and the variations are small.

Communication with the prefecture from mainland Greece is by ferry or by air, and from the other prefectures of Crete by road. The lie of the land and the fact that there are numerous archaeological sites means that a very good internal road network has been created.

The prefecture's capital and by far its largest urban centre is the

Heraklion, view of part of the city. The fortifications at the mouth of the small Venetian harbour are only one of Heraklion's many attractions.

Knossos. View of the site from the air.

city of Iráklio (pop. approx. 140,000) Its older spelling is Heraclion, and historically it has gone by various names: el-Handaq, Khandax, Candia, and Kastro. The city lies on the north coast of the prefecture. It consists of two parts: the Old Town within the city walls, which is the more historic and therefore more rewarding area; and the newer suburbs. Of the many things to see, specially interesting are the 15th-century fortifications guarding the entrance to the small Venetian harbour; the cathedral of St Titus, the patron saint of Crete; the Loggia, an imposing two-storey Venetian building where the nobility used to meet; the church of San Marco, in the Platía Venizélou; and the nearby ornamental Fountain of Morisin, with its lion sculptures. Not on any account to be missed is the great Archaeo-

Phaistos, near the village of Mires. View of the site from the air.

logical Museum; but the city also has various other museums (e.g. the Historical Museum, the Kazantzákis Museum).

Of the remaining historic settlements of the prefecture we would specially recommend Ágios Míronas, Arhánes, Kastéli, Zarós, and Arkalohóri in the central area; and Timbáki, Vóri, Míres, Pírgos, Áno Viáno, and Péfko in the south.

Of the four prefectures of Crete, Iráklio is the most important for the archaeologist, for it was the very centre of Minoan civilization, destroyed in the 15th century BC, probably by some natural disaster. The biggest attraction is undoubtedly Knossós, just south of Iráklio. This was the hub of Minoan civilization for some six centuries (2000-1400 BC). Here we see the reconstructed Palace, and the ramins of shrines, burial monuments, chambers, workshops, and storerooms. You can admire the Throne Room, and, in a copy (the original is in the Archaeological Museum at Iráklio), a fresco of incomparable beauty, the 'Prince of the Lilies'.

Second only to Knossós for its archaeological importance is the site at Phaistós, in the south west of the prefecture and not far from the village of Míres. Here too, the spade of the excavator has brought to light important finds: the Minoan palace, a Middle Minoan tomb, the 'Petit Palais', and 'beehive' tombs. Also found during excavation was the celebrated Phaistos Disk, with its Linear A inscription, still the object of much scientific (and unscientific!) discussion and dispute.

Matala. This is a famous tourist attraction, with its caves hewn in the rock and its long sandy beach.

Not far from Phaistós to the north east, in the Plain of Mesará, is the site of classical Gortys, one of Doric Crete's oldest, most powerful, and best governed city-states. It reached its peak of prosperity during the Roman occupation, only for its traces to be lost in the 9th century AD. There are the remains of sacred and secular monuments; and there is the celebrated Law Code of Gortyn, neatly carved on a wall of massive stones. Another major archaeological site in the prefecture is at Mália, close to the village, on the north west shore. Here were found the remains of a Minoan palace and cemetery, and traces of other buildings. Also of interest are the finds at classical Tylissus, south west of Iráklio, where the remains of three Minoan villas contemporary with the New Palace at Knossós were found.

One last place to visit on this archaeological tour of the prefecture should be mentioned, and that is the Dictaean Cave, on the border with the prefecture of Lasíthi, the birthplace, according to myth, of Zeus.

The prefecture has benefited by extensive development for tourism. Two of the best developed are Liménas Hersonísou, a cosmopolitan resort, and the seaside village of Mália, which in the summer is crowded with young people. Mátala is a tourist destination famous the world over for its caves. Fódele has the house of Dominikos Theotokópoulos, better known as 'El Greco'. Háni Kokkíni and Sindonía are two other resorts worth visiting for the traveller in Crete.

PREFECTURE OF LASITHI

The prefecture of Lasíthi – or more correctly the prefecture of the Plain of Lasíthi – comprises eastern districts of Crete. It is washed by the Sea of Crete to the north and the Libyan Sea to the south east.

The prefecture is nearly entirely (88%) mountain or upland. The most striking feature of its landscape is the broad, fertile Plain of Lasíthi. Its highest massifs are mount Díkti (2148 m) in the west and mount Thrípti (1476 m) in the east. Its water supply is from winter torrents and underground streams. The coasts are heavily indented to the north, with the large open Bay of Mirabéllo and the Spinalonga peninsula. It also has quite a number of offshore islets (e.g. Gaidouronísi, Koufonísi, Elása, Dragonáda). The climate is mild and Mediterranean, but with variations in the mountain regions.

Communication with the prefecture from Athens is by ferry from the Piraeus to Ágios Nikólaos or Sitía, or by air from Athens

Agios Nikolaos. View of the harbour and part of the town.

International Airport. The internal road network has fairly good coverage and is under constant improvement.

The prefectural capital is Ágios Nikólaos (pop. approx. 10,000) on the north west coast of the Bay of Mirabéllo. It has a considerable harbour and many tourist establishments. Among the things to see in the town are the Archaeological Museum and the Folk Museum; the Kondoúreios Library; the Byzantine church of Ágios Nikólaos with its frescoes dating from the 8th or 9th century; and the little lake of Voulisméni. In the neighbourhood (11 km further north) is the cosmopolitan resort of Eloúnda, on the site of classical Olous. Another resort with intensive tourism is the peninsula of Spinalónga, with its Venetian fortifications. South east of Ágios Nikólaos, at Kritsá, are the remains of the classical city-state which Dorians called Lato, and other Greeks called Leto.

As you tour the west of the prefecture, you would do well to take a look at the historic settlements of Neápoli, where there is an archaeological collection; Tsermiádos; the cave of Psíhro, a place where people worshipped in Minoan times; and the Lasíthi plateau

Elounda, a resort village north of Agios Nikolaos.

Spinalonga. On this island the Venetians planted a fort to guard the harbour of Elounda.

Zakros. View of the site from the air. The main feature is the great Minoan palace, built probably in about 1600 B.C. and destroyed a hundred and fifty years later.

with its many windmills, some still in working order.

On the south coast, at the geographical centre of the prefecture, where so to speak the waist of Crete is pinched in to form the narrowest distance between the Bay of Mirabéllo and the Libyan Sea, is the prefecture's largest urban centre, Ierápetra (pop. approx. 15,000). Built on the site of classical Hierapytna, the town is a popular tourist resort. Its attractions include a 13th-century Venetian fort; the Archaeological Museum; and numerous churches including the Panagia Kalé. From Ierápetra it is a short crossing to the lovely island of Gaidouronísi (also known as Hrisí), with its remarkable cedar groves and its exotic beaches.

North of Ierápetra are two major archaeological sites. The first is at Gourniá, with the ruins of a Late Minoan settlement. This was a flourishing city in Minoan times: it has been called a 'Minoan Pompeii'. The second is the nearby village of Vasilikí, where there are equally important finds of monuments (e.g. the 'House on the Hill') from the early days of Crete.

The main urban centre in east Lasíthi is Sitía (pop. approx. 10,000), on the north coast, in the Bay of Sitía. This is a town which is developing its trade and tourism very rapidly, due largely to having both a port and an airport. Here you should visit the Archaeological Museum, which contains a wealth of finds from the surrounding area. Close by are three archaeological sites: at Petrá and at Tripitós (with important settlements from Minoan times) and also at Hamaízi, where there is the one and only 'oval' house of the Minoan period.

Further west, you can go round the impressive Minoan settlement at Palaíkastro; enjoy what is Europe's only palm grove (five thousand palm trees!); and visit the Toploú Monastery and its museum. Venturing further south, there is the spectacular archaeological site of Zakrós to visit, with its Minoan palace.

Your tour of the prefecture might wind up with a journey to the pretty, and deserted island of Koufónisi (also known as Léfki), with its superb landscape and its remarkable antiquities (stone-built theatre, public baths, slag tips, settlement, shrine, &c).

Vai, and its long beach. The district is famous for having the largest stand of palm trees in Greece.

Corfu, view of Palaiokastritsa.
This village on the west coast
is a massively popular tourist
destination with excellent hotels.

IONIAN ISLANDS

PREFECTURE OF KERKYRA

The prefecture of Kérkyra comprises the Ionian island of Kérkyra (or Corfu) (area 592 km²), opposite the shores of Epirus, and of Albania, to the north west; the island complex of Paxoí and Antípaxoi; and a considerable number of smaller islands and islets (the principal of which are Othonoí, Ereikoúsa, and Mathráki).

The island of Kérkyra (or Corfu) forms a rough inverted triangle flattened to the north, and some 62 km long from north to south. The prefecture is two thirds (67%) plain. Its most mountainous profile is in the north, with the Pantokrátor (or San Salvatore) peak (914 m). Kérkyra has no rivers and its water supply depends mainly on winter torrents and underground streams. There is also one lake: lake Korissíon, in the west. The shores are somewhat precipitous in the west, but friendlier in the east. The climate is mild and Mediterranean, and this makes for a rich growth of plants and trees. The island has frequent connections with mainland Greece by ferry and by air. The internal road network is in fairly good shape.

Kérkyra (Corcyra) – very long ago called Drápanos ('sickle') or

Corfu Town. The buildings in the island's capital, many of them listed monuments, are mainly in Western European style. They are a reminder of Corfu's rich history.

Corfu Town, view of the fortress and its installations. These are a very popular tourist attraction.

'the island of the Phaeacians' – was colonized by Corinth in the 8th century BC. Time and again it played a leading part in classical and later history. It was the hatred between Kérkyra and Corinth that sparked off the Peloponnesian War. For centuries afterwards the island was to be occupied by one foreign power after another. In 1386 it fell into the hands of Venice, and the Venetians remained there until 1797. Then came the French, the Russians, the French again, and finally (in 1814) the English. It was England that governed the island, with a wide variety of administrative schemes, until Kérkyra was eventually incorporated into the fledgling Greek state, in 1864. Two melancholy stages in the island's more recent history were its bombardment by Italy, in 1923, and its occupation by the Nazis, from 1941 to 1944.

Kérkyra's history has decisively influenced the island's cultural traditions. Western European influence is much in evidence, and is particularly strong in its spoken dialect, its drama, its music, its painting, and its architecture.

The prefecture's historical and administrative centre is the town of Kérkyra or Corfu (pop. approx. 28,000), is also its main port, on the east coast, a museum of Western architecture unique of its kind in Greece. There is much to be seen in the town and its environs. Particularly interesting are the Agora of classical Corcyra, at Palaió-polis, with its Doric temple of Cardacius, its Roman Baths, the so-called 'port of Alcinous', and the five-aisled 5th-century church of Ágia Kerkyra; the archaeological site at Fináretos near Kanóni; the 15th-century Fort and the New Fortress; the Royal Palace (Mon Repos), once the residence of the English Governor; the Town Hall; the Old County Hall (1835); many Orthodox churches and other monuments (the church of Ágios Spyrídon, the island's patron saint, built in 1589; the Panagía Spiliótissa, built in 1577; the 18th-century Panagía of the Foreigners; the 15th-century St John the Baptist; the 16th-century St Nicholas of the Old Men, and so on). The Palace Gardens at Mon Repos contain a sanctuary of 'Corcyrean' Apollo, offering the visitor a delightful promenade; as does the Achilleum, today a museum and casino, but once the residence of the Hapsburg empress Elizabeth of Austria ('Mayerling') and then of 'Kaiser Bill'. The town has a splendid Archaeological Museum; a Museum of Oriental (previously of Chinese and Japanese) Art; a Solomos Museum and a Kapodistria Museum; a Museum of the National Fight for Independence, housed in the historic building where the Ionian Parliament used to sit; a Museum of Ceramics; and a Paper Money Museum. The town's beautiful central square is known as the Spaniáda. On it is the Listón, a complex of several-storey buildings with an arcade and wall lanthorns, providing locals and tourists with a meeting point.

From Kérkyra you can visit Lazaréto, a pretty island developed for tourism. Or you can tour the delightful eastern coast, with obligatory stops to the south at Benítses and Lefkími, and to the north at Potamós and Kassiópi. On the north coast you should not miss Sidári, and on the west coast is famous, cosmopolitan Palaiokastrítsa.

You can also go across the water to Paxoí, the name of the island and of its main town (also called Gaíos), where you will find a wealth of natural beauty and the celebrated sea caves known as the *graves*.

View of Paxoi. This is a lush island of great natural beauty, with the celebrated sea caves known locally as 'grava'.

PREFECTURE OF LEFKADA

The prefecture of Lefkáda comprises the Ionian island of Lefkáda (area 302 km²) plus a substantial number of adjacent small islands and islets, mainly to the south east (e.g. Meganísi, Kastós, Skorpiós, Spárti, Petalú, and Kíthros). The north east part of the prefecture, in which lies the town of Lefkáda itself, all but touches the shore of the prefecture of Aitoloakarnanía. This allows of easy access, by a bridge.

The island is irregular in shape. Its northernmost point is the headland of Girópetra. To the south are the two headlands of

Nidri, on Lefkada. This village on the east coast has become the main holiday resort on the island. It is the perfect combination of lovely scenery, excellent hotels, and a cosmopolitan atmosphere.

Doukáto and Lipsó. The prefecture is three quarters (78%) mountain or upland. The highest massif is mount Stavrotá, with its peak Eláti (1167 m). The coasts are heavily indented, especially to the south and east, and are frequently sheer cliff, especially to the west. The island has no rivers, so that the main source of water is its subterranean streams. Its climate is mild and Mediterranean, favouring the growth of forest and forest plants.

Communication between Lefkáda and the remainder of Greece is by road. The prefecture's capital, after which it is named, is 380 km from Athens and 480 km from Thessaloniki.

Lefkáda – Santa Maura, as it was known historically – was reunited with Greece in 1864. Its history dates back to the Middle Palae-

olthic Age. Over the centuries it was occupied by one foreign power after another, the last being Britain, which attached Santa Maura to the Ionian Islands. It has also suffered heavily from earthquakes, the worst being that of 1953. Culturally it is akin to the rest of the Ionian Islands in having been much influenced by Italy and Western Europe. It does however show a number of differences: these are due partly to the fact that it was the one island in the region to come under Turkish rule (for more than two hundred years), and partly to its geography (it is a very close neighbour of Mainland Greece). Lefkáda's individuality is particularly evident in the way its people speak, their music, their folk dress, and their manners and customs.

A good place at which to start a tour of the island is its capital (pop. approx. 7000). This is in the north, almost opposite the mainland shores of Central Greece. During the summer months it is a popular and lively destination for tourists. The town is picturesque in appearance, with traditional single-storey and two-storey mansions: it has a good hotel infrastructure. Particularly worth seeing are the Castle of Santa Maura, dating from about 1300; the Central Public Library, with its rare books from the 15th century; the churches of Ágios Spyrídon (1685) and Christ the Omnipotent (1684); and the seafront promenade, with its adjacent lagoon, now an important biotope.

Of outstanding interest among the monuments on the island are the Bronze Age burial mounds at Stenó, not far from Nidrí; the classical Agora near the seaside village of Póros on the south east coast; and to the west Évgiros, with its traces of Neolithic civilization. The main religious monument to visit, the island's monasteries apart, is

The little isle of Madouri, on Lefkada. Shown here is the house of one of the great Greek national poets, Valaoritis.

the 15th-century Byzantine church of the Panagía Odigítria, at Apól-paina, 2 km from Lefkáda town. Of more recent buildings, particularly rewarding is the Valaorítis family mansion on the islet of Madourí.

The island of Lefkáda is a real paradise for green tourism. There are scenic routes along the west coast (Kariótes, Nikiána, Nidrí, Póros), the south coast (the harbourages at Roúda, Aftéli, Kastrí, Vasilikí), and the west coast (cape Doukáto, and the beaches at Atháni, Drágano, Kamíli, Kalamítsi, Ágios Nikítas, Tsoukaládes, &c). There is an enchanting route inland by way of Kariá, Platístoma, Sívros, and Síbota. It is also very pleasant to go for a jaunt among the offshore islands, the main ones being Meganísi (with its villages of Vathí, Spartohóri), Kálamos (with its villages of Kálamos and Episkopí), and Kastós.

Lefkada, view of Porto Katsiki. In this imposing landscape, the sandy beach is screened by a sheer rock cliff.

PREFECTURE OF KEFALONIA

The prefecture of Kefaloniá (the form Kefallinía is also found) comprises the Ionian island of Lefkáda (area 782 km²); the much smaller island (area 96 km2) of Itháki (the classical Ithaca); the islets of Arkoúdi and Átokos; and the islet chain of the 'Spiny Ones', the Ehinádes, offshore of the prefecture of Aitoloakarnanía.

The island is irregular in shape. The line of its coast features four large bays, the Bay of Sámi in the east, the Bays of Loúrda and Argostóli in the south, and the Bay of Mirtó in the north. Itháki lies to the north west, the two islands being separated by the Strait of Ithaca. The coasts are heavily indented, for example the bay of Mólos. Both islands have by and large a mountainous profile. There are peaks at Aínos (1628 m) on Kefallinía and Níritos (806 m) on Itháki. The prefecture has adequate water, thanks to winter torrents

View of Argostoli. This town, the capital of the prefecture of Kefalonia, lies on the Gulf of Argostoli, and has a considerable harbour.

and underground streams. Its climate is mild and Mediterranean, favouring the growth of plants and trees.

Communication between Kefaloniá and Itháki and mainland Greece is by ferry and by air. The prefecture's road network is adequate and under continuous improvement.

According to myth, Kefallinía got its name from Cephalus son of Theseus. In the course of the years it was to know many an over-lord, including Venice (1500), France (1797), Russia (1798), France once more (1806), and England (1814). The latter incorporated it into their autonomous protectorate state of the Ionian Islands (1815). It was reunited with Greece in 1864. In 1953 it suffered ter-rible damage from the great earthquake that struck the Ionian region as a whole. Similar was the history of Ithaca, Homer's 'home-land of Odysseus'.

The prefecture's capital and largest town is Argostóli (pop. approx. 10,000), lying on the gulf of the same name, with its sub-stantial harbour. The town had to be almost entirely rebuilt after the great earthquake. It has broad squares, fine public buildings, and the Pavement, a pedestrian precinct of traditional type where there are shops and cafes popular with the young. Among the things to see in Argostóli and its environs are the Korialenios Library, in which is housed the vitally important Historical and Folk Museum; the archaeological museum; the great causeway linking Argostóli with the other side of the gulf; the lagoon at

View of Lixouri. It was in this town on the west coast of the Gulf of Argostoli that the poet Lascaratos was born.

Kefalonia. The fine beach at Mirtos, in the north west of the island.

Koútavos; a scientific celebrity, the Katavóthres (swallowholes); and the cave of St Gerasimos, in which this patron saint á, with a rare books collection; the Laskarátos Monument; the Venetian castle, now in ruins; and several historic monasteries. Three seaside resorts with long sandy beaches are Mégas Lákkos, Xi (the mysterious X!), and Kounópetra, named for a large and precariously balanced rock.

From Argostóli you can make south east to the imposing Castle of St George, the island's original capital, and thence to the eastern shores. Here you will find some charming villages: Skála, Póros (with its 'Dragon's Cavern', of great archaeological interest), Sámi, and the delightful fishing village and summer resort of Fiskárdo, a conservation area. Further north west still, on the north coast of the island, lies the isthmus of Ásos, with its Venetian castle. This is one of the most charming corners of a charming island.

You are also recommended to explore the slopes of mount Aínos, with their wealth of natural beauty.

The principal town and main port of Ithaca (Itháki) is Vathí (pop. approx. 2000), in the south. It has the traditional Ionian Island style of architecture: little low houses with tiled roofs and colourful doors and windows. The archaeological museum should not be missed, and there are the ruins of a Venetian castle.

The island has some lovely spots: the Marmarospiliá ('marble cavern'), thought by many to be Homer's 'Grotto of the Nymphs', in which Odysseus stowed away the gifts he had been given by the Phaeacians; Aetós ('eyrie'), with prehistoric antiquities; Perahóri (with the Taxiarchón Monastery); the Katharón Monastery on the slopes of mount Níritos; and Stavrós, where there is an archaeological collection. It also has the pretty seaside villages of Kióni and Fríkes, with their little harbours and windmills.

Ithaca.

PREFECTURE OF ZAKINTHOS

The prefecture of Zákinthos comprises the island of Zákinthos (420 km²), 8.5 sea miles south of Kefallinia and 9.5 sea miles west of the north coasts of the prefecture of Ilia. It also includes some offshore islets.

The island is an irregular triangle in shape. Its northernmost point is the Skinári headland, and its southernmost points are the Marathá headland, to the west, and the Geráki headland, to the east. Between lies the great Bay of Laganás, with its islets of Marathonísi and Pelúzo.

The island is semi-upland. Its highest mountain is Vrahíonas (756 m.). It has no rivers and its hydrographic system consists mainly of underground streams. The coasts have a tendency to end in sharp capes and little inlets, more so in the west than in the east and south. The climate is mild and Mediterranean, making for a rich flora. Zákinthos is of particular interest to ecologists because the southern shores of Laganas Bay have become a Greek national Marine Park where the loggerhead turtle (*C. caretta*) comes to lay its eggs.

Zakinthos Town. View of the harbour from the castle.

The island's west coasts are also home to another protected species, the Mediterranean monk seal (*M. monachus*).

Care has been taken to maintain good transport connections with mainland Greece, principally through the mainland harbour opposite at Kyllíni. There is also an air link with Athens and also Thessaloniki, from the airport not far from the main town; and many charter flights come in from abroad. The island's internal road network is under constant improvement.

Zákinthos – the 'Flower of the Levant' (*Fior di Levante*) as it was known to the Italians – is a place with a long history, a rich cultural tradition, and rare natural beauty. It was already inhabited in prehistoric times. Its founder according to legend was Zakynthos, son of a king of Phrygia, Dardanos. It is mentioned in the Homeric poems, where it is described as thickly wooded. It occurs frequently in classical and later texts. In more recent times it was often conquered, and at other times ravaged by earthquakes. In 1185 it fell into the hands of the Franks; in 1479 it was annexed by Venice; between 1797 and 1809 it shuttled between French and Russian occupation, after which it became a British protectorate, as part of the autonomous Ionian Isles (1815). It was reunited with Greece in 1864.

The island's fortunes are reflected in its culture, where Western influence is uppermost. This can be particularly seen in literature: from Zákinthos have come such great writers of mixed tradition as Solomos, Ugo Foscolo, Kalvos, and Xenopoulos. Also noteworthy have been the Ionian School of playwrights, and leading figures in music (the *kantádes* of Zákinthos are famous), painting, and vcernacular architecture.

The prefecture's main focus, as an administrative centre and as a port, is the town of Zákinthos (also called Hora), with a population of around 17,000. This is on the east coast, with a sizeable harbour. It and much of the island suffered massive damage as a result of an earthquake and the fires which followed it, in 1953. Most of the churches and public buildings were levelled to the ground. In the next few years there were painstaking efforts to restore the town and its historic buildings, particularly the harbour and the historic squares named for Solomos and for St Mark. We would mention the Castle (actually a composite structure of various periods), the churches of St Dionysius (the island's patron saint) and St Nicholas on the Quay (which escaped major damage), and the Roman Catholic church of St Mark. The Prefecture Hall and the Law Courts now house the town's two major museum collections, namely the Museum of Post-Byzantine Art and the Museum of Solomos and Other Great Zakinthians. Other sites of interest are the

←

Zakinthos, Navagio ('Wreck'). This isolated spot can be reached only from seaward, by boat. It takes its name from a wrecked ship that was washed ashore there.

Zakinthos Town. The statue of one of the great Greek national poets, Solomos.

picturesque suburb of Bóhali, and the hill of Stráni, where Solomos was inspired to write his *Hymn to Freedom* (the Greek National Anthem).

Also 'essential viewing' are such impressive settlements on the island as Vanáto, Mahairádo (with the adjacent monastery of Agia Mavra), Pantokrátoras, Katastári, and Volímes. You should if possible explore the whole of the enchanting shoreline, with its pretty seaside villages, and its wonderful facilities for swimmers, fishermen, and nature-lovers. Names to look for are Xirokástelo, Argási, Vasilikó, Plános, Alikanás, and Askós, on the east coast; the Blue Cave in the far north; Navágio, Kambí, Agalás and Kerí on the west coast; and of course Laganas Bay, four or five miles from the main town and a cosmopolitan summer resort crowded with visitors.

TABLE OF CONTENTS